Building a Better
International NGO

Building a Better International NGO

Greater than the Sum of the Parts?

James Crowley and Morgana Ryan

Kumarian Press

A Division of Lynne Rienner Publishers, Inc. • Boulder & London

Published in the United States of America in 2013 by
Kumarian Press
A division of Lynne Rienner Publishers, Inc.
1800 30th Street, Boulder, Colorado 80301
www.rienner.com
www.kpbooks.com

and in the United Kingdom by
Kumarian Press
A division of Lynne Rienner Publishers, Inc.
3 Henrietta Street, Covent Garden, London WC2E 8LU

ISBN: 978-1-56549-582-1 (cloth: alk. paper)
ISBN: 978-1-56549-583-8 (pbk.: alk. paper)

Library of Congress Cataloging-in-Publication Data
A Cataloging-in-Publication record for this book
is available from the Library of Congress.

British Cataloguing in Publication Data
A Cataloguing in Publication record for this book
is available from the British Library.

Printed and bound in the United States of America

The paper used in this publication meets the requirements
of the American National Standard for Permanence of
Paper for Printed Library Materials Z39.48-1992.

5   4

Alzheimer's
Research UK
Defeating Dementia

The net proceeds from this book are being donated to Alzheimer's Research UK. As the second-largest charity funder of dementia research in the world, we are at the heart of global efforts to defeat dementia. The research we fund offers the greatest hope, bringing us closer to finding ways to diagnose, prevent, treat, and cure dementia. Everyone who buys a copy of this book will give hope to the millions of people across the world living with dementia today.

More than 35 million people worldwide are estimated to live with Alzheimer's disease or another form of dementia. Each year 4.6 million new cases are diagnosed and that number is set to spiral, bringing massive social and economic pressure to bear. The lack of funding for research makes dementia a global health time bomb. It is only through the combined efforts of governments, the public, and the dementia research field that we can avert a worldwide dementia catastrophe.

—Rebecca Wood, Chief Executive, Alzheimer's Research UK
www.alzheimersresearchuk.org

Contents

List of Tables

List of Figures

Chapter 4

Chapter 5

Chapter 6

Chapter 7

Acknowledgments

The authors would like to offer their deep thanks for invaluable input, feedback, and suggestions on early drafts particularly from:

Christine Allison, Independent Development Consultant, formerly of the World Bank

Ian Anderson, Deputy Board Chair, Oxfam Australia, former Chair, Oxfam International; Coauthor of "Tomorrow's Inclusive Development"

Tom Arnold, CEO, Concern Worldwide

Craig Barry, former Director Finance and IS, Oxfam Australia

Carol Bothwell, Chief Knowledge Officer, Catholic Relief Services (who provided an invaluable contribution to Chapter 4, and who continues to provide tremendous leadership in the sector in relation to ICT4D)

Grahame Broadbelt, Director, Tomorrow's Company

Karen Brown, Chair of Trustees, Oxfam GB

Gib Bulloch, Executive Director, Accenture Development Partnerships

Chris Carrigan, CEO, Esteliant

Lord Nigel Crisp, Chair of Sightsavers (former CEO of UK National Health Service)

Ian Curtis, Partnership Lead for Governance, World Vision International

Jim Emerson, Secretary General, ChildFund Alliance (former COO and CEO of Plan International)

Jo Ensor, Director of Philanthropy, Charities Aid Foundation (formerly Chief Executive of AMREF UK)

Matt Foster, Head of Strategy and Performance and Regional Director of VSO International

Robert Glasser, Secretary General, CARE International

Burkhard Gnärig, Executive Director, Berlin Civil Society Center

Ian Gray, Associate Director Policy and Programme Innovation, World Vision UK

Professor John Hailey, Centre of Charity Effectiveness, Cass Business School, City University

Susannah Hares, ARK (formerly head of programs at AMREF UK)

Sherine Jayawickrama, The Hauser Center for Nonprofit Organizations, Harvard University

Kevin Jenkins, President, World Vision International

Ryan Johnson, Director, Cross-Sector Engagement, Catholic Relief Services

Chris Jurgens, Director, Global Partnerships, USAID

Paddy Macguinness, Managing Director, Traidlinks

Catherine Marsh, Production Support, Accenture

Marg Mayne, CEO, VSO International

Charles McCormack, Senior Fellow, Inter Action

Tom Miller, former CEO, Plan International

Muhammad Musa, CEO and Country Director, CARE India

Annemarie Riley, Head of Strategy and Performance, Catholic Relief Services

Darius Teter, Vice President of Programs, Oxfam America

Marcy Vigoda, Deputy Secretary General, CARE International

Tosca Bruno-van Vijfeijken, Transnational NGO Initiative, Syracuse University

Ian Wishart, CEO, Plan Australia

The Accenture Development Partnerships team, in particular Louise James, Dee Jadeja, Rachel Manton, Lionel Bodin, Ian Lobo, Roger Ford, Jessica Long, Dan Baker, Sarah Glass, Anastasia Thatcher, Trip Allport, Paul Chadha, Matt Radford, Angela Werrett, and Tina Senior

And especially:

Deborah Crowley, Chief Editor, ably assisted by **Aisling** and **Rebecca.**

A Short Note from the Authors

Many thanks for taking the time to explore our ideas and recommendations on the subject "greater than the sum of the parts." The journey to producing this book began over three years ago based on a combination of frustration on the one hand and a desire to contribute on the other. We were frustrated by some common challenges and organization blockages that seemed, all too frequently, to get in the way of some really talented people in excellent organizations contributing the most that they could. On the other hand, after seven-plus years, engaged with a range of NGOs at all levels, we felt that we should and could make a small contribution toward expediting progress for those who are already strengthening their international organizations or prodding complacent organizations into reflection and hopefully action.

Throughout these reflections, we have tried to be careful and thoughtful in how we have positioned our challenges. We want to be respectful of the great progress many organizations are making to improve. However, we also want to issue a clear call for action, to ensure that organizations that have contributed enormously over the past several decades, and have grown impressively in recent times, will continue to stay relevant and contribute to much-needed breakthroughs in the years ahead. While there are many reflections, ideas, and suggestions throughout this set of chapters, there are three central messages that we would like to draw to your attention:

- First, a range of external changes and opportunities calls for a **reevaluation of each NGO's role and contribution to the development process.** This is driven by factors such as continuing globalization, evolving thinking on good development practice, the need for local ownership of solutions, the growth in interest of private sector organizations, as well as exciting new possibilities through technologies of all kinds. This is required in order for

NGOs to stay focused, be good at what they do, and be reliable partners in the ongoing fight against poverty.

- Second, every international NGO (INGO) has both **the opportunity and the obligation to strengthen and modernize its organization and management approach at an international level.** These changes need to encompass structures, mind-set, management style and capacity, skills, processes, and systems. It is imperative that agencies be able to respond to the dramatic growth in scale and scope of activity and resources, the evolving nature of poverty and its impacts, the expanding scope of interventions, and the growing imperative to work alongside an increasing array of other important partners. The basic structures and management approach that still characterize many INGOs will not suffice into the future.

- Finally, what is required is not just a transformation of efficiency and effectiveness. Yes, relentless efforts to improve efficiency are needed to eliminate waste and duplication at all levels of the organization and to utilize modern technology and ways of working. Yes, INGOs need to become more effective, which means designing and implementing the best programs they know, all of the time, while adapting to local contexts for maximum impact. However, this is just the foundation. The real prize is in the **discovery and exploitation of major breakthroughs, removing blockages and exploiting new possibilities in the fight against poverty and injustice.** Creating breakthroughs involves the organizational space and energy to utilize knowledge, insight, and connections across the entire organization, as well as with other agencies and stakeholders to come up with innovative breakthroughs that will really change the color of the map. Small-scale incremental progress is useful, but it will not get us where we need to be.

Large established INGOs have a strategic choice. They can muddle on with an ever-expanding scope of activities and an organization model that is based on "business as usual," designed for the needs of the past. If they pursue this route, they will risk becoming marginalized or superfluous in the years ahead. Alternatively, INGOs can take the next step in strengthening their organizations, being very clear with their strategic focus, and becoming truly great organizations in terms of the contribution they make, as well as great partners to work alongside.

This book is not intended to give a definitive answer or a specific way forward for any individual NGO. While we do draw from experience and developments from the private sector, we do not intend to imply that INGOs should become exactly like private sector organizations. We also accept and expect that some might not agree with all of our ideas or suggestions. The intention is to prompt deeper reflection and also to provide some frameworks, ideas, and suggestions to help management have a more productive review of their particular situation and to prepare to make the best strategic choices for the future.

There is no perfect sequence to the chapters; different topics may relate to particular challenges of different organizations at any particular time. Hence, they can be read in any order depending on your situation. However, when an INGO is contemplating a global strategic review in the near future, we would hope that all of the chapters have some relevance to stimulate its preparation.

We would especially like to thank those organizations we have had the privilege of supporting over the past seven years. In particular we acknowledge World Vision (International and World Vision UK), Plan (International, Plan UK, and Plan Australia), AMREF (African Medical and Research Foundation), VSO (Voluntary Services Overseas), Catholic Relief Services, Amnesty International, The Asia Foundation, Oxfam (International, Oxfam GB, Oxfam Novib, and Oxfam Australia), Save the Children (International, Save the Children UK, and Save the Children Australia), Habitat for Humanity International, the International Rescue Committee, and CARE International, whom we have the opportunity to assist in a fascinating range of strategic assignments. We also thank a range of individuals, many from these organizations, who have provided invaluable input and reaction to earlier drafts of our ideas.

To conclude, we are delighted to offer the net proceeds of this publication for the benefit of Alzheimer's Research, a cause that Morgana and I feel receives far too little attention and investment in light of the challenges it presents to both those directly affected and their families.

Good reading!

—**James Crowley and Morgana Ryan**

Introduction and Overview

The "Sum of the Parts" Idea

Giving to a good cause is sometimes an impulsive act for an ordinary individual. It is implicitly a decision of trust that gives a certain gratification to the giver, with an expectation that the money will provide relief, hope, and maybe some progress to someone, somewhere, near or far. At an institution, foundation, or corporate level, the process of giving has many of the same traits, but of course one expects it to be more sophisticated and hopefully more rigorous.

International development and relief agencies (often referred to as international NGOs [INGOs]) provide a way to give assistance to the poor and disadvantaged in the developing world. Many came into being during the middle part of the past century by extraordinarily committed people who opened up the possibility for us all to help. These organizations set up programs, typically at grassroots level, in the poorest areas of the world, helping with issues such as water and sanitation, food insecurity, education, health and agriculture, and relief from famine and disasters, natural or man-made. As funding and programs have expanded and multiplied, many INGOs have expanded their operations and now work in up to one hundred countries, with operating budgets on the order of $1 billion to $2 billion a year for the largest. They have a complex network of offices at field, regional, and central locations, as well as income-generating offices in many countries in the richer parts of the world. All of these offices need to be coordinated at a global level through some form of international management approach and supervised by an international secretariat or headquarters. All this takes a good deal of time, resources, and investment to make it all work.

However, these international development and relief agencies are not the only ways for donors to channel their contributions. There are also many opportunities to contribute directly to numerous small local charities, such as local orphanages, schools, or small local country-based NGOs. One can give, for example, through a church, which in many cases has established structures and capacity on the ground in many poor countries—meaning that any contribution can be channeled in full to the front line, since the infrastructure already exists and is most likely already fully funded. And increasingly, with new possibilities in the age of the Internet, one can connect directly with community organizations and local businesses in the developing countries, either as direct giving or directly investing through new investment channels such as kiva.org.

So what is the rationale for channeling one's contribution through the big international agencies such as Oxfam, World Vision, or Save the Children? Yes, these organizations have deep expertise, are staffed with professional development workers, and have an incredibly strong network of relationships with local communities, local and national governments in poor countries, and a range of donors. They are well equipped to match resources to areas of need. They have a well-trained workforce to implement the programs they design, working closely with local communities and other stakeholders. However, we are obliged to ask the $100 million question: **Are large INGOs delivering a contribution that is greater than the sum of the parts?**

Introduction to the "Sum of the Parts" Research

There is no doubt that large INGOs have developed and matured over the past ten to twenty years. They have had to undergo many changes in order to continue to be relevant and effective in the pursuit of their aims. In many ways they have made great progress.

First, they had to extend their reach to address new areas of conflict and need. They have expanded their range of interventions to tackle new problems such as HIV and AIDS and, more recently, the disproportionate impact of climate change on poor and developing countries. They have had to evolve and strengthen their programmatic approach, the core of how they do their work to adapt to the lessons and failures of the past. This has required a deliberate move away from a charity-based approach toward being much more facilitative and supporting, with a stronger emphasis on human rights, and ensuring genuine local ownership of problems and solutions.

INGOs have also begun to collaborate much more seamlessly with local bodies, community-based organizations and with local and central governments. More recently, they have even been encouraged to work in tandem with the private sector, which had traditionally been regarded as the "dark side" by many in the NGO community.

And, of course, there is the ever-growing clamor to demonstrate concrete evidence of the long-term impact of NGOs, be it in terms of achieving the United Nations' Millennium Development Goals or other metrics of progress set out by increasingly demanding donors.

There has indeed been very considerable progress, yet we know that inside many large INGOs, things are not always as one would hope or expect. Despite some encouraging progress in recent years, some large INGOs have difficulty operating as genuinely global organizations; the components sometimes feel like distant cousins within the same warring clan. When you speak to managers and staff within these organizations, you frequently hear comments such as the following:

- Decision making is too slow and consensual.
- There is considerable inefficiency or duplication across the different parts of the organization.
- There are disjointed ways of working, disjointed processes, disjointed decisions, and disjointed initiatives across the organization.
- Individuals in their local node of the organization are overly protective of local perspective and unable or unwilling to see the bigger picture of the whole.
- Stakeholders at headquarters make decisions without understanding the realities of work in the field.
- Leadership behaviors are not always a shining example; criticisms on occasion include a lack of humility, respect, and management discipline.
- We're not making as much impact as we could or should.

Why is this? Why do INGOs face such challenges in operating as global organizations? Is it something intrinsic to the sector, something that we have to accept? For example,

- Is it inevitable given the strains of constantly working in unstable, changing environments?
- Is it related to the constant uncertainty regarding long-term sustainability of their funding sources?

- Is it a by-product of balancing the demands of donors' requirements and expectations with the needs of those on the ground whom INGOs seek to help?
- Or are INGOs, even the largest ones, spread too thin, in too many countries, covering too many domains of activity?

This last issue is particularly acute for many INGOs that are today challenged with the pressures of very dramatic growth over the past decade. Some INGOs, for example, have seen a doubling or trebling of their income over a relatively short period.

Like any other international organization spanning a range of countries and business areas, INGOs should consistently strive to ensure that the whole is indeed greater than the sum of its parts. That means, in simple terms, that the benefits of being part of a broader international organization should exceed, in aggregate, the costs and efforts of coordinating and managing the global organization.

We know that the costs associated with activities such as management time and coordination efforts, as well as investments in common processes, systems, or standards, can be very significant. This is not surprising given the very wide range of activities of many large INGOs in terms of range of geographies (up to one hundred countries in some cases), breadth of domains (health, education, microfinance, agriculture livelihoods, governance, and so on), and the numerous types of interventions and partners that are involved. And, of course, the scale of activity on the ground in a typical program country is usually quite modest. A US$20 million budget for an INGO in a developing country is still regarded as relatively large in many cases. These overhead and coordination costs become less significant, however, where the scale of activity is very large and where the magnitude of the synergies that arise as a result of being part of a bigger international family is considerable.

In the private sector, where diseconomies of scale and scope exceed economies and synergies, disposals or demergers ultimately take place. While INGOs are not exposed to the same market forces as the private sector in relation to mergers, acquisitions, and divestitures, there is an equivalent management and moral pressure to ensure that the whole is indeed greater than the sum of its parts.

This brings us back to the key question in this research: **Are large INGOs delivering a contribution that is indeed greater than the sum of their parts? In other words, are the economies of scale and scope greater than the implied additional costs of management, coordination, alignment, and integration** for an INGO? If we are in doubt, what is a pragmatic way forward to ensure that this is the case?

This series of chapters explores this central question from six different, though complementary, perspectives. They are intended to provide food for thought, to provide lenses to understand and dissect some of the important issues, and to suggest some potential ideas and recommendations.

As we tackle this set of issues, we acknowledge the considerable efforts that several large INGOs are making to bring greater cohesion and effectiveness to their global organizations. We cite the "unified presence" and subsequent initiatives by Save the Children International and equivalent efforts by Oxfam International, to name a couple. We also applaud the ongoing efforts of NGOs such as World Vision and Plan International, which already benefit from a unified organization in all of their program countries and have been working hard to strengthen their global leadership and management structures, as well as some of their most strategic systems. The World Wildlife Fund and others are making valuable progress with the implementation of integrated and professional performance and accountability frameworks across all of their entities across the globe.

However, for many INGOs we know the challenges are considerable and there is much yet to do. We have had the privilege of assisting with a number of strategic planning reviews, as well as a range of other strategic assignments, for several large and very large international agencies over the past seven years. Through this work, we can observe some remarkable consistency in the kinds of big strategic questions that emerge and demand attention, for example:

- What, in the future, should be the scope and real focus of our contribution to reducing poverty and helping to deal with emergency situations?
- What specifically are we really good at, and what do we really need to be good at to deliver our mission?
- What is our *theory of change*, that is, our shared understanding of how positive and sustainable social and economic progress occurs, to best effect, in poor countries?
- How do we reflect the dramatically changing possibilities from ICT (information and communication technology) in how we design and implement our programs?
- Is our organizational model and structure right today, and is it equipped to deal with the demands of the future?

- How do we operate more effectively as a global organization?

These questions became the central lines of interrogation in this research process and map directly on how we have structured our analysis and observations in this book.

Overview

The first chapter, "Getting in Shape: How to Make a Large International NGO Be More Than the Sum of Its Parts," looks at the question from the perspective of organization models, power, decision making, and management process. How can these large organizations operate in a synergistic, cohesive way and ultimately in a manner that ensures that the whole is indeed greater than the sum of the parts? This analysis identifies twelve key factors or prerequisites that we believe are particularly important for large international agencies.

In the second chapter, "Good at What? The Core Competencies of International NGOs: What Are They? What Do They Need to Be?" we take a step back and explore what INGOs are really good at and need to excel at to have the impact they desire. The chapter argues that agencies need to be much more precise and disciplined in understanding and nurturing their core competencies to have a useful role in the future. The chapter questions whether it is still credible and effective to be a "jack of all trades" in the development process, across so many differing contexts, in fifty to one hundred countries, spread across three or four continents.

The third chapter is titled "Evolving Structures of International NGOs: Is There a Right Answer?" and looks specifically at the issue of INGO structure, reviewing structural options and variants in the context of evolving thinking on organizational structures over the past century. We reflect on the learning and emerging wisdom from efforts to improve effectiveness of organizations in the private sector over the past few decades. We argue that the simple geographical structure, which has been the common form for many agencies, is no longer equipped to deal with the challenges of the future. However, leadership behaviors and approaches will need to transform in parallel with any changes to structural form.

The fourth chapter, "Reinventing International NGOs Th rough New Technology Possibilities," explores the possibilities that modern technology provides in rethinking and potentially reinventing the role, contribution, and ways of working of INGOs in the development process. We also explore whether the changes through information and communications technology could be "sustaining" technologies for the work of large international agencies or, alternatively, "disruptive" technologies that could result in the demise of the large international agencies we know today unless, of course, they transform and adapt.

The fifth chapter is titled "Strategic Planning for International NGOs: Reflections and Perspectives." This chapter is intended to help get the most out of a strategic planning process and to avoid some of the common pitfalls. The success factors and approach are based on our extensive experience of strategic reviews in the private sector as well as on our hands-on experience helping with major strategic reviews with a number of large international development and relief agencies.

The sixth chapter is titled "Integrated Planning and Accountability for International NGOs." This chapter is intended to expand on an important area of weakness that is highlighted in some of the earlier chapters. This chapter sets out some practical ideas on what a professional framework could look like, as well as describing some important considerations when implementing a new approach.

The seventh and final chapter, "What Does All This Mean?" seeks to bring together the essence of the previous six chapters and to articulate the key reasons why large international NGOs need to embrace change. We summarize some brief comments on navigating change. We also describe a somewhat provocative and maybe controversial view of the sector in 2024—which is undoubtedly going to be wrong. This projection is merely intended to provoke some deeper reflection on what the sector might look like in the future.

We fully appreciate that each agency will have its own particular history, context, and direction that will make the right recommendations different for each specific situation. However, we feel that INGOs are now at a point of inflection in terms of their role and contribution as the world is a different and rapidly changing place. They need to adapt, focus, and transform if they are going to continue to be central to the fight against poverty. We hope that this material will provide a useful reference for the journey.

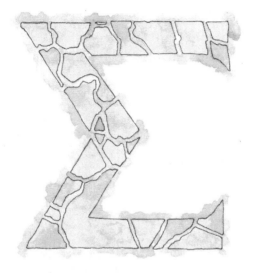

1

Getting in Shape

How to Make a Large International NGO Be More Than the Sum of Its Parts

Abstract

This chapter was written for senior executives, CEOs, chairs, and active board members of large international NGOs (INGOs) who are concerned about the added value created by the international functions and structures. The chapter has, at its core, two simple ideas. The first is that it should indeed be possible for large INGOs to make a contribution that is far greater than the sum of their parts. That is the good news. The bad news is that there are considerable blockages and challenges to be overcome, and it may take relentless focus, determination, and humility over a long period of time to become a truly excellent high-performing international organization.

In this chapter we seek to diagnose the context, major issues, and challenges. In our analysis, we explore the match of different organizational models with different contexts, paying attention to the tension between the pressures for local responsiveness on the one hand and the benefits of global coordination and integration on the other.

We identify twelve important requirements that we believe can help large INGOs have an impact that is greater than the sum of the parts. A number of these speak directly to the need to move on from what we refer to as the "relational," "line of sight," or "command and control" management approach. The journey toward a more professional, transparent, and objective management approach is a unifying theme across many of the requirements.

These requirements are structured into three groupings or themes. The first of these is the theme of **programmatic legitimacy**, which at its core means that all programs that are supported by an agency, at either a local, a national, or an international level, follow a clear and aligned view of good development practice. We draw attention to four aspects of programmatic legitimacy, namely, quality local programs, alignment around a *theory of change*, ruthless clarity and alignment on organizational core competencies, and finally capacity, contribution, and impact at an international and global level.

The second theme relates to **operational maturity**, which is centered on the management and enabling processes, as well as management capacity and behaviors. Under this theme, we draw attention to the importance of the mind-set of "dual citizenship," the need for selective alignment of essential enabling processes, and the importance of a single, integrated planning and accountability framework across the entire organization.

The final theme relates to **credible leadership and governance**. We draw attention to the need for a single, integrated global leadership team, the logic for adopting some form of matrix management approach, though one that is aligned with management and process maturity. We refer to the benefits of a distributed/virtual headquarters. We look in some depth to the challenge of workable regions and put forward the merits of smaller, strategic mini-regions with interlinked contexts and programs. Finally we make some comments on the issue of the "North–South" power balance.

1.1. Introduction

For INGOs, the search for an optimal international organizational configuration or model is one that has gone on for many decades and continues today to generate considerable argument and tension. The debate tends to encompass a range of factors, though most frequently it is related to issues of power, control, and decision making. It can also be closely connected to the natural tension that exists between the need for local control and responsiveness by country organizations on the one hand and the desire to exploit the full value of the scale and scope of benefits of being part of a global organization on the other.

One frequent area of tension is between national organizations, often in the North, who typically have their own independent boards and structures and generate very considerable local funding but also are integral parts of large global NGO families or networks, be they federations, confederations, or loose affiliations. A particular issue, for example, relates to the uses of the funds that are collected from individuals and institutions in their country. These national organizations often have an understandable desire to have direct control over how these funds are used in the field, based on concerns around cost efficiency, program effectiveness, and demonstrating accountability to local donors.

However, while these local pressures are very understandable, there is also a range of issues that demand attention from the totality of the organization and need to be addressed if the benefits of being part of a global organization are exploited. For example, the international management of large INGOs is concerned with issues such as

- being more responsive to unpredictable emergencies around the world
- meeting donor demand for greater accountability
- taking advantage of the potential of economies of scale in recruiting, fund-raising, and programming
- maintaining legitimacy of the organization across multiple countries
- exploiting opportunities for greater impact through worldwide organizational learning
- being more accountable to a wider set of audiences and stakeholders
- working out whether, and how, to pursue advocacy activities at local, regional, and international levels

- exploiting the opportunity to use new technology, for example, for coordinated international advocacy
- and last, but not least, achieving more results with less.

Almost a decade ago, this debate was very usefully captured in the book *Going Global*, by Lindenberg and Bryant.[1] This analysis, which included an in-depth survey of a range of INGOs, made a considerable contribution to this debate and identified five broad organization configurations.

These categorizations have become the established language in the debate on organizational models of large INGOs and, in many ways, are a good reflection of what still exists today. However, it is clear that many agencies have evolved through a number of alternative variants subsequent to the original research.

As a reminder, their five classifications were as follows:

- **Unitary, corporate organizations,** where there is only one global organization with a single board and central headquarters, which makes most resource acquisition, allocation, and program decisions (e.g., Catholic Relief Services).
- **Federations,** where the center has strong powers for standard setting and resource allocation, but affiliates have separate boards and implementation capacity (e.g., World Vision).
- **Confederations,** where strong members delegate some coordination, standard setting, and resource allocation duties to the central office, though decisions from the center need virtual unanimity, and most power remains with the larger affiliates (e.g., Oxfam International or CARE International).
- **Independent organizations with weak umbrella coordination,** where independent organizations maintain virtual autonomy but establish a weak coordinating mechanism to share information and facilitate cooperation (e.g., Médecins Sans Frontières).
- **Separate independent organizations,** who share a common name without surrendering any decision-making authority to international headquarters (perhaps Caritas).

This debate has continued to become more complex as INGOs have grown rapidly, expanding their geographical footprint, and the mix of programmatic interventions continues to expand and evolve. Agencies are also seeking to learn from the lessons and failures of the past; a good example of this is the trend toward more emphasis on rights and citizenship and less on resource intensive, service delivery activities such as building and running schools and clinics.

The debate has continued to evolve, for example, through the preference of some large INGOs such as World Vision and ActionAid to move toward granting full membership status to program countries, giving them increased local autonomy and ultimately allowing them to establish their own local, independent boards.

We can observe that many of the large INGOs have evolved and are continuing to evolve their international configurations. This reflects the increasing desire to benefit from the value of being part of a global family while being appropriately responsive to local context and pressures in developing and developed countries. If we continue to follow the evolutions of the international configurations of World Vision, ActionAid, Médecins Sans Frontières, CARE, and more recently Save the Children and Oxfam International, we can see that the search for more effective models continues. In fact the exact classification of any agency is challenging, as most continue to evolve, some moving toward greater coordination and alignment and others in the opposite direction.

1.2. Analyzing Organizational Models

Tension Between "Global Integration" and "Local Responsiveness"

Tensions in large international organizations can sometimes be simplified into two competing forces, namely, the need for local responsiveness on the one hand and pressure for global coordination and integration on the other. This tension is summarized in the matrix in figure 1.1, and a selection of industry sectors are mapped as an illustration.

It is not difficult to see that different types of industries tend naturally to occupy specific quadrants of this global integration–local responsiveness matrix. For example, you can see that for chemicals or oil and gas, the pressure for global integration tends to dominate because of the considerable economies of scale that prevail, as well as the "commodity" nature of the product. For sectors such as legal services or retailing of food and beverages, local responsiveness tends to dominate.

Matching Different Organizational Models to Context

Following on from this line of inquiry, one can begin to explore the link between the various quadrants on this grid with the appropriateness of different organizational models.

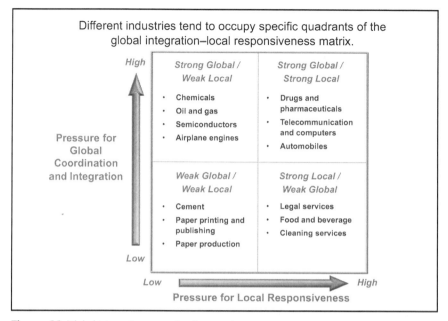

Figure 1.1 Global integration versus local responsiveness.

The diagram in figure 1.2 shows how different organizational types broadly map onto this spectrum. We can see that there is a very strong correlation between the choice of organizational model and the positioning of the industry sector on this simplified two-by-two matrix.

For organizations in the top left quadrant, power and control is oriented toward the headquarters or product dimensions. In contrast, for organizations where local responsiveness is paramount, more power tends to move to the business unit level. The matrix model is often used where there is a strong need to seek the benefits of both global integration and local responsiveness. It is a difficult balance, but if it is managed correctly, the advantages are significant.

Dual Pressures Facing International NGOs

As for the private sector examples, there is an interesting challenge for INGOs because of the considerable imperatives both for local responsiveness on the one hand and for global coordination and integration on the other. Pressure for local responsiveness is strong, particularly within developing country contexts where it is imperative that NGOs are responsive to the needs of local communities. They need to involve communities in decision making about

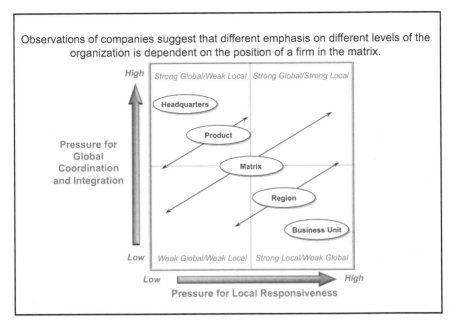

Observations of companies suggest that different emphasis on different levels of the organization is dependent on the position of a firm in the matrix.

High

Strong Global/Weak Local | Strong Global/Strong Local

Headquarters

Product

Pressure for Global Coordination and Integration

Matrix

Region

Business Unit

Low

Weak Global/Weak Local | Strong Local/Weak Global

Low   High

Pressure for Local Responsiveness

Figure 1.2 Matching organizational models to context.

the community and work to help them to understand their rights. They also need to work very closely with the state, civil society, and private sector entities. And of course, they need to be responsive to the broader social and political context; working in India is very different from working in Tanzania, which in turn is very different from working in Sudan. In the more affluent, developed world, where much of the income generation happens, there is also a strong pressure for local responsiveness because of local political, social, and consumer cultural norms.

However, the pressures for stronger global integration are also strong and increasing, motivated by a range of drivers such as those mentioned in the introduction to this chapter. We are also seeing the emergence of a greater international dimension to development programs, for example, around efforts to deal with a range of regional health challenges, as well as agriculture and physical infrastructure development. Another interesting example is the growing importance of advocacy and campaigning activities spanning multiple interconnected countries.

On the funding side, the growing significance of some of the extremely large international donors is also strengthening the need for global integration (e.g., the Gates Foundation, the Global Fund, or the European Union). These donors, while on the one hand increasingly delegating decision making to be closer to program countries, are also seeking to support larger scale, multi-country initiatives. That means INGOs need to be able to access funding at multiple levels and manage programs on a larger and more complex scale than in the past.

Overview of Analytical Framework

However, we needed to extend our analysis to a deeper and more operational level. We approached this analysis using a number of frameworks and theories, starting with the very powerful ideas of Goold and Campbell in *Strategies and Styles*,[2] a book that explores the different kinds of relationships that exist between the corporate center and the businesses or entities within a corporation.

We then revisited findings from an earlier detailed research study[3] that extended Goold and Campbell's thinking into a more concrete level of detail through analysis of a range of well-known global organizations such as Shell, ABB, Vodafone, McDonald's, and others. This work explored where the real control was held for each of the main processes or activities at different levels of an organization.

This investigation became the anchor of our analytical approach. It provided a useful framework for understanding the shapes of different organizations, questioning how, for example, the organizational shape for McDonald's fast-food chain differed from that of ExxonMobil, or indeed Vodafone. What was it about the business context and nature of what one organization did that makes one shape or style work for it but not for another? Later in this chapter, we will extend this approach to INGOs and their particular context and explore what insights and conclusions can be drawn.

To begin, we will briefly describe this analytical framework. There are typically four commonly observed decision-making levels present in the structure of all major international organizations (see figure 1.3). They are consistent regardless of corporate strategy, although for each organization these levels may differ in degrees of importance. There is typically an understandable tension between the four major levels of the organization given competing pressures and perspectives at each level. These organizational levels are as follows:

- headquarters level
- region level
- product or line of business level—this could be akin to domain or particular kinds of programs for INGOs

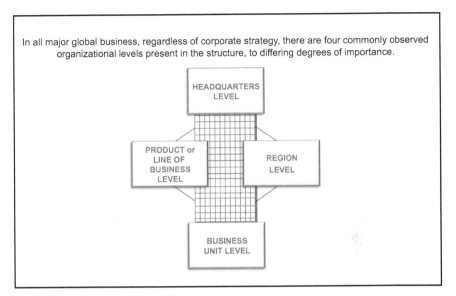

Figure 1.3 The four organizational levels.

- business unit level—sometimes, though not always, equivalent to the local country operation

The second major dimension of the analytical framework looks at the four major groupings of business activities or processes within a major international organization. These are as follows:

- crafting strategy and leading the business
- building the business
- supporting operations
- running operations (day to day)

Each of these groupings contains important business processes or activities that exist in varying ways at different organizational levels of the business, as can be seen in figure 1.4. It is then possible to analyze where activity is located and, particularly, where the key decision-making "center of gravity" lies. This will first be described for some private sector organizations and then more specifically for INGOs. Figure 1.4 illustrates this approach for a large international company called ABB in the 1980s, which owned and managed a variety of businesses on a global scale and was much studied at that time.

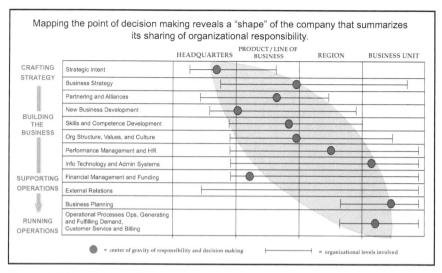

Figure 1.4 Example shape of a private sector organization.

The horizontal lines indicate which organizational levels are involved in each process. The solid dot on each horizontal line indicates where the center of gravity of power or decision making was for that process at the time of the original study. Mapping the points of decision making reveals a shape of the company that summarizes its sharing of organizational responsibility.

From the example in figure 1.4, you can see that headquarters had little or no involvement in many of the processes. Its main point of engagement was primarily with issues around strategic intent, corporate strategy, and new business development.

You can also see that there was considerable power vested in both the regions and the lines of businesses, in order to respond to the specific characteristics of the markedly different types of businesses ABB owned in its overall portfolio, as well as the varying requirements of different regions. These "middle" levels were also important because of the relatively small size of the individual business units in each of the countries—requiring that economies of scale around performance management, HR, financial management, and partnering and alliances were driven from a region or line of business level.

The business units had considerable autonomy around all operational processes, albeit with some input at a regional level where there were obvious economies of scale within similar businesses.

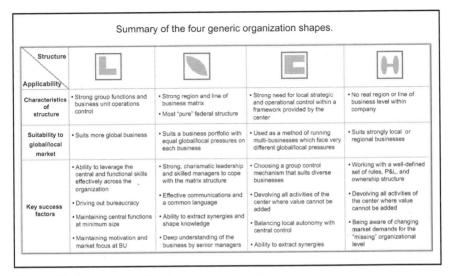

Structure / Applicability	L	Diagonal	C	H
Characteristics of structure	• Strong group functions and business unit operations control	• Strong region and line of business matrix • Most "pure" federal structure	• Strong need for local strategic and operational control within a framework provided by the center	• No real region or line of business level within company
Suitability to global/local market	• Suits more global business	• Suits a business portfolio with equal global/local pressures on each business	• Used as a method of running multi-businesses which face very different global/local pressures	• Suits strongly local or regional businesses
Key success factors	• Ability to leverage the central and functional skills effectively across the organization • Driving out bureaucracy • Maintaining central functions at minimum size • Maintaining motivation and market focus at BU	• Strong, charismatic leadership and skilled managers to cope with the matrix structure • Effective communications and a common language • Ability to extract synergies and shape knowledge • Deep understanding of the business by senior managers	• Choosing a group control mechanism that suits diverse businesses • Devolving all activities of the center where value cannot be added • Balancing local autonomy with central control • Ability to extract synergies	• Working with a well-defined set of rules, P&L, and ownership structure • Devolving all activities of the center where value cannot be added • Being aware of changing market demands for the "missing" organizational level

Summary of the four generic organization shapes.

Figure 1.5 Shapes observed in private sector organizations.

Shapes Observed in the Corporate Sector

While there are many nuances and features that make generalization difficult (in the same way there are differences within the INGO sector), the research revealed four broad shapes. These shapes are set out in figure 1.5, as well as some of the associated characteristics and success factors related to each shape.

The "L shape" is typified by truly global businesses, where local pressures are less important than global advantages of scale and standardization. The "diagonal shape" is typified by businesses where global and local pressures are both important and where region and line of business dimensions play a useful role, providing a manageable way of ensuring the advantages of international scale on the one hand while providing reasonable flexibility in responding to local needs on the other. This is more typical where a company is involved in many different kinds of businesses.

The "C shape" suits organizations where there are significant global economies of scale, but the dual local and global pressures mean there is equal sharing of decision making at the strategy-setting level and also at the operating level. A good example of this is a global consulting organization such as Accenture, where there is considerable local flexibility at the business unit level in terms of which products and markets to pursue but within a clear global template that is coordinated at a region and/or line of business level. There is also a lot of flexibility at the local level in terms of project implementation, though it is often based on a standard approach or methodology. The areas that are mandated, and hence are not negotiable, include key human resource management policies and processes, performance management processes, business performance standards and targets, and organizational values. In addition, adherence to the global knowledge management approach and procedures is a mandated process for all staff wherever they sit in the organization.

As we reflect on this particular shape, it is interesting to note that there are notable parallels between the knowledge, people, and program-based organizations such as Accenture and large international development agencies, which might make this particular shape worthy of further consideration.

The "H shape," typified by organizations such as Visa, the financial services company, tends to suit businesses working in a narrow business focus, with strong global-scale economies but also with very strong local business pressures. There are minimal region and line of business levels within the company. The key success factor here is for a stable business model that is equipped to work with a well-defined set of rules, profit and loss (P&L), and ownership structure.

Adapting the Analytical Framework for International NGOs

So what can be gleaned by examining the structures of large INGOs using a similar framework and approach? To retain as much comparability as possible, we stayed as close as possible to the same framework. However, there are a few necessary refinements to reflect the specific nature and characteristics of INGOs (see figure 1.6).

The organization levels have been slightly refined to reflect some of the specific governance models one can observe. First, we divided the headquarters column into two subcolumns to reflect the distinction between international "headquarters/secretariat" level and the "lead entity" level characterized by INGOs such as CARE International and Oxfam International.

The business unit is also subdivided to distinguish between business units of a mainly programmatic nature (field/country programs) and country offices that are primarily concerned with fund-raising.

For the activity/process breakdown, the same four broad groupings of processes (craft strategy, build the business, support operations, and run operations) are still used. Where it does vary is in some of the underlying processes. These refinements are outlined in the adapted framework and shown in figure 1.7.

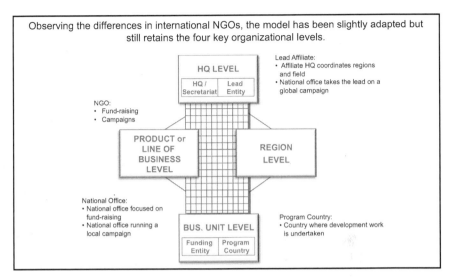

Observing the differences in international NGOs, the model has been slightly adapted but still retains the four key organizational levels.

Figure 1.6 Four levels, adapted for international NGOs.

		HEADQUARTERS		PRODUCT/ LINE OF BUSINESS	REGION	BUSINESS UNIT	
		HQ/Secretariat	*Lead Entity*			*Prog. Country*	*Predominantly Funding Entity*
CRAFT STRATEGY	Global strategic planning						
	Country strategic planning						
	Partnerships and alliances						
BUILD THE BUSINESS	Brand development and management						
	New opportunities and business dev						
	Skills and competence development						
	Org structure, values, culture						
	HR and individual performance mgmt						
	Finance and procurement						
	IT systems						
	Internal and external relations/comms						
SUPPORT OPS	Risk management/assurance						
	Knowledge management						
	Bus planning and performance mgmt						
	Marketing and fund-raising						
	Research						
	Program: Development						
	Program: Campaigning/advocacy						
RUN OPS	Program: Humanitarian						
	Monitoring and evaluation						

Figure 1.7 Revised framework for international NGOs.

Having made these slight adjustments to the approach to accommodate the realities of an INGO, we then conducted a mapping for a range of organizations. Admittedly, this work is based on external perspective and does not purport to know in detail all of the internal specifics of every NGO.

The processes listed in figure 1.7 are at a summarized level and in certain areas, it was necessary to extend the mapping to the subprocess level to get to a more meaningful level of understanding and insight.

However, in this chapter the mapping is summarized at the highest level only, and it is possible to draw some interesting observations at this level to prompt useful insight and debate. Organizations considered included INGOs such as Oxfam International, World Vision International, AMREF (African Medical and Research Foundation), Amnesty International, Plan International, VSO International (Voluntary Services Overseas), and CARE International.

Before going on to discuss the emerging shapes from the analysis, we fully acknowledge that a number of these organizations are undergoing significant internal change and restructuring, and the picture observed is, at best, a snapshot at one point in time.

1.3. Organizational Shapes for International NGOs

General Observations

What can we deduce from the shapes that emerge in broad terms? Clearly, there are some particular differences across organizations because of their history, their structure, the nature of their programs, and their footprint. Figure 1.8 shows a broad and somewhat simplified profile for a generic INGO. Before going on to look at the typical shapes that can be observed, it may be helpful to use this simplified example to summarize some general themes that emerged during the analysis of the various INGOs considered.

Illusion of Widespread Participation With Multiple Levels of Decision Making
At a surface level, we can observe somewhat of an "illusion" of heavily aligned organizations with many levels having a say in the design and execution of most processes. In the framework, this manifests itself as many extended horizontal lines, in a way that was not the case in the commercial examples. For many processes, we can observe decision-making nodes at the center and also in both the field and the funding offices. The result could be regarded as a "veneer of participation" where all parts of the organization seem to be involved in decision making for the majority of processes (or at least are seen to be). The reality, however, is that many of the processes are weak or in some cases are

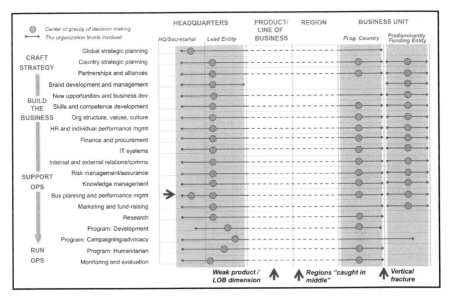

Figure 1.8 Profile for a generic international NGO.

running completely independently in two or three parts of the organization. So much "surface-level" integration and participation can, unsurprisingly, cause much frustration. As a consequence, it is not unexpected that organizational agility can sometimes seem to be a challenge.

Vertical "Fracture"

For a number of NGOs, there seems to be a clear break between the processes that relate to the programmatic part of the organization (at the center and left of chart) and those processes centered on the mainly "Northern" based funding offices. These units often operate their own set of processes, which have been developed and evolved to meet local needs over time. This means that integrated planning and resourcing trade-offs are difficult and contentious, and decision making about longer-term investments to strengthen the backbone of the organization becomes problematic.

Scale, or Lack Thereof, Is a Critical Constraint

Even the largest INGOs cannot afford the cost of full alignment and integration across all of the processes and activities that make up an INGO, nor should they try to. It is simply too costly to create, implement, maintain, and enforce a complete set of fully aligned processes and IT systems. This issue is of particular relevance as strains emerge as a result of the very meteoric growth (often doubling or trebling in income) experienced over the past decade. The issue is also challenging because of the lack of willingness of most donors to provide funding for what seems like overhead cost, or nonprogrammatic, activity.

Large INGOs are now in a difficult situation in that they **are too big to be small and too small to be big.** Covering the full spectrum of development domains, across 50 to 100 countries on three continents, is an enormous scope for organizations that have, in reality, fairly modest operating budgets. This characteristic makes identifying the essential "glue" all the more important. (As an aside, it is our view that many NGOs are far too thinly spread across far too many countries. Most would provide significantly more in terms of contribution and impact if they were to reduce the number of countries they function in by between a half and a third.)

Regions Are Often "Caught in the Middle"

For organizations with such a broad range or scope of activities, the role of regions or lines of business seem to be relatively minor. Regional offices sometimes appear to be mere extensions of headquarters, nodes of management that do little more than reduce span of control. In some cases they attempt to provide shared technical expertise or support services or even carry out regional programs. However, in many cases, the sheer number and range of countries covered means that the feasibility of providing real value added to country programs can be limited.

In reality, regions are sometimes caught in the cross fire between the need for local responsiveness at the program country level, local responsiveness at the funding entity level, and greater global coordination desired by the center. Hence, they often end up responding to many different stakeholders with very little ability to effectively influence the activities of the organization.

In our conclusions in section 1.4, we probe deeper into the key components of the role of regions and suggest a pragmatic, though perhaps somewhat controversial, way forward.

Lines of Business Often Lack Backbone

In reality, lines of business are often informal networks of people focusing on program areas or domains. They may have similar interests, but they sometimes lack rigor, continuity, and strategic focus. Typically, they do not have a formal place in global management processes and hence end up filling a role more akin to a "debating" mechanism or, at best, a "community of practice" and are not fully integrated into the organizational fabric.

There are, of course, some innovations and very encouraging developments within some agencies. A good example is CARE's "Access Africa," which is a pan-Africa Centre of Excellence around microfinance. Country-level microfinance teams now have dotted-line reporting to this programmatic center of excellence. This is enabling CARE International to have a much stronger local and international competence in the area of microfinance.

Weak Planning, Performance Management, and Accountability Processes (the Last Days of the Relational Style Management Approach)

Another interesting observation is that planning, performance management, and accountability processes for INGOs are often too weak and narrow, subjective, or just not helpful enough. The traditional relational style of management, which is characterized by strong historic personal relationships, line of sight supervision, and in certain cases command and control, is no longer appropriate for the modern, professional, and larger-scale INGO. This area is especially difficult to address quickly and needs to be tackled with patience. This dilemma was eloquently described in this famous quote, attributed to Einstein: "The level of thinking which got us to the current state is not sufficient to deal with the problems and shortcomings that arise from that state." Indeed, a lack of interest in, appetite for, or habit of management discipline may be a contributory cause to many of the other challenges we can observe for INGOs.

Where Is the Real Glue?

When you look across the various organizations, it can, in some cases, be difficult to isolate the "essential glue" that is really binding the organization together to ensure that the whole is greater than the sum of its parts. The strict operating procedures of McDonald's; the strategic and financial discipline of ABB; the HR and performance management discipline, project methodology, and knowledge management emphasis of Accenture; and the ubiquitous planning and organizational performance management disciplines of ExxonMobil are all examples of real organizational glue. Some INGOs will rightly point you to their unifying purpose or values, which are, no doubt, important, but is this "motivating glue" alone sufficient?

On a practical level, some INGOs are just coming to grips with issues such as common financial years and standard financial terminology, so it is little wonder organization-wide integrated planning and operations can sometimes seem a challenge. Others have been challenging themselves to reach consensus on their understanding of development "good practice" with regard to, for example, the essential characteristics of an effective and sustainable

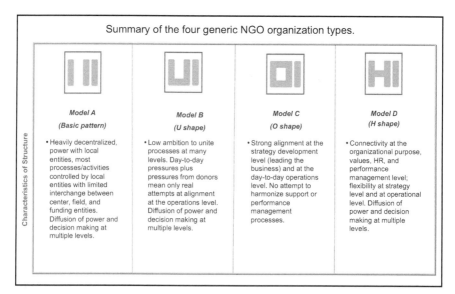

Figure 1.9 Observed NGO organizational shapes.

development program. These are all basic requirements to become a coherent global NGO and ones we will dwell on further in section 1.4 of this chapter.

Four Observed Shapes

When we looked across all of the INGOs reviewed, what emerged was a variety of shapes, which were all variations of the same underlying theme. These are illustrated in figure 1.9. Figure 1.10 sets out the same information in a slightly simplified manner, with an emphasis instead on levels of integration across each of the process areas. The three vertical bars in Model A illustrate the three main levels of decision making across the majority of processes. There is strong local responsiveness but limited benefits from being part of a wider organization. There is limited "glue" to foster knowledge exchange and leverage the full might of the organization to achieve potential economies of scale.

In Models B, C, and D, you can see the emergence of more integrated processes, though at different levels. In Model B, the emphasis on real integration is at the programmatic/operational level, with few serious attempts at integration at the strategic level or at the middle support process level. This could be described as the pragmatic model, where management accepts that more serious integration is just too problematic and does not merit the effort and investment.

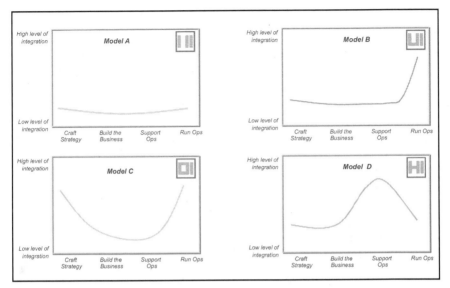

Figure 1.10 Integration points for different international NGO models.

In Model C, there is an attempt to seek additional integration at the higher strategic levels, though again with little real effort at integration at the middle-level processes. In Model C, we can see the challenge of high integration around strategy and running operations but without the facilitation provided by processes around planning and supporting operations. (However, one could challenge, for example, how effectively staff from two or more entities can work together on program activities if they cannot access common information or systems, have different planning and budgeting cycles, or are on hugely different terms and conditions.)

Model D is different as it allows much more autonomy at the strategic and day-to-day operational levels but seeks to integrate around organizational values, as well as key support processes such as finance, HR, and business performance management. Model D illustrates a situation where organizations have seen the benefits of integration around support operations as a means to enable greater local responsiveness in other areas.

What is interesting about all four shapes is that the diagonal shape discussed earlier for a number of diversified organizations in the private sector was not evident for INGOs. **We feel that INGOs that want to remain multisectorial and also cover a broad range of geographies might do well to consider this diagonal shaped model.** That would suggest pushing responsibility for building the business and supporting the business away from headquarters and into the control of more focused strategic regions, as well as to distributed lines of business.

An alternative shape is the C shape from the private sector. This form seeks to balance the dual local and global pressures at both the strategy-setting level and the day-to-day operating levels while seeking deeper alignment and standardization at a few key areas, for instance, around talent management, organization planning and performance management, HR, knowledge management, and program methodology. This conclusion is supported by the interesting parallel between the dynamics of development agencies and those of professional service firms such as Accenture or PwC. In both cases the key assets are people, knowledge, talent, and cumulative learning and methodology, as well as deep relationships with those customers and stakeholders that the organization serves.

1.4. Conclusions and Recommendations

Can the whole be more than the sum of its parts? Having reviewed the shapes of a range of INGOs and considered their structures and decision-making patterns, we identified a number of very important requirements that we believe can help large INGOs have an impact that is greater than the sum of the parts. These are what we believe to be the glue elements, the points on which INGOs can seek to have greater integration without taxing limited resources and shifting focus from the things that matter most. A number of these speak directly to the need to move on from what was earlier referred to as the relational, line of sight, or command and control management approach. The journey toward a more professional, transparent, and objective management approach is a unifying theme across many of the requirements.

Core Requirements

This list of requirements follows on directly from the conclusions of the shapes analysis in previous sections. However, we fully acknowledge they are also informed by our practical experience working with a range of INGOs over the past several years, as well as previous exposure to the workings of large international organizations in the private sector. These requirements are structured into three groupings or themes. The first of these is the theme of **programmatic legitimacy**, which at its core means that all programs that are supported by an agency, at either a local, a national, or an international level, follow a clear and aligned view of good development practice. We draw attention to four aspects of programmatic legitimacy, namely, quality local programs, alignment around a theory of change, ruthless clarity on organizational core competencies, and finally capacity, contribution, and impact at an international level. We will expand on each of these areas later in this section.

The second theme relates to **operational maturity**, which is centered on the management and enabling processes, as well as management capacity and behaviors. Under this theme, we draw attention to the idea of dual citizenship, the need for selective alignment of essential enabling processes, and the importance of a single, integrated planning and performance management framework across the entire organization.

The final theme relates to **credible leadership and governance**. This theme speaks to the selection of an organization model and the associated leadership and decision-making structures. Attention is drawn to the need for a single, integrated global leadership team and the logic for adopting some form of matrix management approach, though one that is aligned with management and process maturity. The benefits of a distributed/virtual headquarters are also considered. We look in some depth to the challenge of workable regions

Programmatic Legitimacy

1. Quality local programs with sustainable impact
2. Alignment around a theory of change and programmatic approach
3. Ruthless clarity and alignment on organizational core competencies (current and future)
4. Capacity, contribution, and impact at an international/global level

Operational Maturity

5. Mind-set of dual citizenship
6. Essential global processes aligned at a sensible level
7. Integrated organizational planning, performance, and accountability (end of relational management approach)

Credible Leadership and Governance

8. Single, integrated global leadership team
9. Matrix management approach aligned to management and process maturity
10. Distributed "virtual" headquarters
11. Strategic mini-region with interlinked contexts and programs
12. North–South power balance; sensible, representative governance

and put forward the merits of smaller, strategic mini-regions with interlinked contexts and programs.

Program Legitimacy

This theme of program legitimacy embraces four important suggestions.

Quality Local Programs With Sustainable Impact

One of the important initial assumptions is that the debate on being greater than the sum of the parts is relevant only if the parts are robust, that is, local programs are of a very good quality in terms of design and implementation, with strong evidence of impact and sustainability. This is the essential foundation of a high-performing INGO, and though it is not the central focus of this series of research chapters, we feel the point needs to be highlighted at the outset.

Alignment Around a Theory of Change

The next requirement is for genuine and deep alignment across the international organization on how positive and lasting change comes about in developing communities, countries, and regions. That includes, in simple language, a shared understanding of the most important ingredients or characteristics of a high-quality development program. Most organizations find it relatively easy to gain consensus on statements around purpose and vision; however, deep alignment on a theory of change or, more simply stated, what good development practice means in reality can be more challenging. Without this, alignment and cohesion will be difficult across many day-to-day issues and decisions.

In fact, the debate around theory of change has not been as center stage as one might expect for organizations that are mainly about stimulating and expediting change. Unsurprisingly, misalignments often exist between funding offices and field program functions in terms of what donors are willing to support and what might be regarded as good development practice on the ground. However, misalignment also often exists between key staff in field programs whose views have, understandably, been shaped by their own personal experiences and beliefs.

Of course, achieving alignment should not and need not be at the detriment of ongoing learning. In fact, in our view, having a shared perspective and methodology provides a key foundation for ongoing learning and sharing.

The problem in this area is accentuated within some INGOs by an overreliance on external freelance consultants who are seen as the only ones with the necessary expertise and capacity to design good programs. That, in our view, is detrimental to organizational learning.

Ruthless Clarity and Alignment on Organizational Core Competencies

With a rapidly changing landscape in terms of perspectives and opportunities for governments, the private sector, and local and international agencies, we believe that development agencies need to reconsider their role and specific focus.

We argue that the idea of core competence, if properly and deliberately thought through, is potentially a very productive way to help large NGOs achieve a more valued and sustainable strategic focus, increase their contribution and impact, and establish a credible source of comparative advantage into the future. It can help clarify which capability investments are most important for the future and help spawn new innovative programs and products that are based on core competence. It can also enable other organizations to see more clearly where and when to partner with you.

The management debate around strategic focus, which is often articulated in terms of choices around geography or sectors, might more productively be conducted around core competencies. This recommendation is the subject of chapter 2 of this book, which is specifically dedicated to this topic and is titled "Good at What? The Core Competencies of International NGOs."

Capacity, Contribution, and Impact on an International/Global Level

In an increasingly interconnected world, collaboration with local community-based organizations, state institutions, and civil society within program countries is now broadly accepted as necessary but not sufficient. A number of the challenges to alleviate poverty require cross-border attention, needing solutions at international as well as at local and national levels to achieve sustainable progress. Without international presence and carefully designed international initiatives, the work NGOs carry out in individual communities and countries will have less chance of achieving maximum desired impact.

These could, for example, be advocacy orientated (influencing policy and practice) though not exclusively so. Programs could address pan-country health issues or livelihood issues in regional zones. Other examples could include connection and influence with regional political forces such as the Southern African Development Community (SADC), the G20, the European Union, and the United Nations bodies. It could also include connection with new powerful forces such as China in relation to Africa and with trade and protection issues, which are a major barrier to progress for many poor countries.

In a world of limited resources, if you extend this premise to its natural conclusion, one could deduce that INGOs would consider drawing back from countries where they have small or isolated programs in order to be able to have a more substantial influence at multiple levels in strategic regions.

Operational Maturity

This theme of operational maturity embraces three important suggestions.

Mind-set of Dual Citizenship

One of the frequent observations of newcomers to the development sector is how territorial staff and leaders are about their own office, country, or function. This is a feature that we have found to be much more pronounced in INGOs than in the private sector. Managers and staff across NGOs need to become comfortable with the notion of dual citizenship (the ability to wear two or more hats) and see each decision or trade-off from multiple perspectives where appropriate.

Thankfully, the idea of dual citizenship is gaining traction in a number of organizations where individuals are asked to take on responsibility for global roles, in addition to their local responsibilities. Managers can take on a global role, irrespective of where they are located, meaning the central headquarters becomes diffused throughout the organization. A good example of this is World Vision's move a few years back to a more "virtual" international leadership structure.

Essential Global Processes Aligned at a Sensible Level

One of the real insights from the shapes analysis is how different the profiles for the INGO sector are compared with the larger companies in the private sector. The extreme complexity of INGOs with their huge geographic and programmatic spread and limited people and financial resources represents a significant point of departure between INGOs and private sector organizations. It is sometimes possible to see evidence of a pervasive lack of trust, which is not common to the same extent in the private sector. The consequence of these factors is that for NGOs it seems multiple levels of the organization feel the need to have an input to and/or control of many processes and decisions. That can lead to frustration, lack of progress, lack of responsiveness, and unnecessary cost.

INGOs should look to identify the essential processes that need to operate on an international or in some cases global basis and then determine the appropriate level of consistency. Is it sufficient to have consistent policy but variations on how things are done? Is it necessary to have the same underlying procedures and IT systems? The deeper the level of integration, the greater the investment required. We believe that hard decisions have to be made to identify where alignment should be and to what degree. In many cases the headquarters needs to let go and allow regions, lines of business, or local offices to make the necessary decisions. At the same time, there is also a need to allow, in some key points, greater levels of organization-wide standardization. In fact, we believe a new kind of "line of business" emphasis needs to emerge with responsibility clearly set as a formal part of the international management process and led by the best individuals, who could well be located in the field or as close to it as possible.

Where it is essential to have aligned processes, one node of the organization needs to take the lead. That requires that entities can accept a situation that may be less than 100 percent ideal for their specific needs or historical practices but is better for the organization overall. Obvious processes that may justify some level of coordination or integration include program design (toolkit and methodology), monitoring and evaluation approaches, knowledge management, finance and accounting, and human resource and talent management.

Integrated Organizational Planning, Performance, and Accountability (End of Relational Management Approach)

One of the key priorities to emerge from our analysis is the need for integrated planning, performance, and accountability. This will be a critical facilitator in becoming a "joined up," aligned organization. It can help ensure that objectives and success criteria are transparent and that the contribution of every part of a global organization is explicit and aligned with the organizational goals. It can also help to ensure that the voices of key partners and the communities in which we work are heard and integrated into the ongoing management discussion. All this will support the aim of jointly maximizing the performance and contribution of everything the agency does.

That does not imply complex systems or reams of reports. It does imply the need for alignment on some very summary and critical performance information, embracing metrics such as program quality and impact, people, money, and stakeholder satisfaction. An associated and very essential part of this requirement is the need for discipline and management process to create a forward-looking, constructive, and nonsubjective management and learning environment.

As indicated earlier, this requirement speaks directly to the need to move on from what we earlier referred to as the relational, line of sight, or command and control management approach. This journey toward a more professional, transparent, and objective management philosophy is a unifying theme across many of our recommendations and is discussed further in chapter 6, titled "Integrated Planning and Accountability for International NGOs."

We fully appreciate that this journey is not an easy one and that it will take time and patience to achieve the right approach for this sector and for each individual organization. It will always be challenging because of the fragmented governance structures of many INGOs, as well as the unique nature of the work in this sector. However, we feel that it is a journey that is both achievable and essential.

This transition is very much aligned to Kaplan and Norton's "balanced scorecard" concept as described in their classic textbook *The Balanced Scorecard*[4] and *Harvard Business Review* articles.[5] Over the past twenty years, this kind of approach has become standard practice for major international organizations in the corporate/private sector. It is gradually appearing on the agenda of INGOs, and some are making encouraging progress, though to date very few have embedded it into their DNA.

Credible Leadership and Governance

This theme of credible leadership and governance embraces five important suggestions.

Single, Integrated, Global Leadership Team

Large INGOs cannot operate well using a command and control approach. The emphasis on planning, performance, and accountability set out above is not to strengthen command and control but to allow the organization to take collective ownership of its progress and performance in a transparent and professional way. That needs to be facilitated by a strong and broad-based leadership team, which represents all of the most important dimensions of the organization. This team needs to look across the total organization to bring all of the entities of the agency together to make decisions for the good of the whole.

Irrespective of the set of legal and formal governance structures in place, it is impossible to operate as a global organization where the whole is greater than the sum of its parts without the existence of a single and well-functioning global leadership team that is able to take critical decisions on behalf of all the stakeholders, both internally and externally. The alignment and discipline of this team will make it easier for all parts of the organization to deliver on their own remit.

This global leadership team should draw from the best talent and expertise across the entire organization, irrespective of where it formally sits or its physical location. Members must be able to think and act as dual citizens and take difficult decisions that may result in sacrifices for their individual entity for the benefit of the whole. This concept also requires that local boards have empowered their senior leaders to take this attitude when participating in organization-wide senior leadership teams. We believe the existence of a global though dispersed leadership team is good practice and can be enabled by good communications technology to minimize travel and cost. It is now standard practice in equivalent knowledge-based organizations in other sectors. It should be noted that this requirement links very closely with the idea of "dual citizenship" identified earlier.

Matrix Management Approach, Aligned to Management and Process Maturity

Many of these suggestions imply the adoption of some form of matrix management, which became both popular and controversial in the 1980s and 1990s but has now (despite its critics) become standard practice in most large international organizations. It is as relevant to INGOs as it is to big commercial organizations. It does not mean there is not clear accountability for results. It does mean the management processes recognize the very important dimensions that need coordination, nurturing, and management. Dimensions might include, for example, geography (regions and countries), lines of business, and areas of skill/expertise.

The issue of structural alternatives, including the matrix management approach, is the subject of chapter 3 in this book, titled "Evolving Structures of International NGOs: Is There a Right Answer?"

Distributed/Virtual Headquarters

We believe that the notion of a large high-profile headquarters located in the North is a concept that will not endure. We envisage the trend toward more diffused and pervasive leadership and management structures: North and South. These will be integrated on a global basis and staffed with individuals who are virtual in location and in many cases as close to the field as possible. This concept will be considerably helped when approaches to integrated planning, performance, and accountability processes mature from their current status as ideas or "works in progress" to become "business as usual." It will also be helped by ongoing improvements in information and communications technology, which will make remote working approaches more feasible and effective over time.

Strategic Mini-Regions With Interlinked Contexts and Programs

Regional organizational levels are important and sensible dimensions of large international organizations, though they can prove to be problematic for some large INGOs. We believe there are two key issues that contribute to this.

First, the design of regions is often influenced excessively by "top-down" logic, that is, what seems like a sensible span of control from the perspective of headquarters, and not enough by "bottom-up" context and needs (e.g., what is a sensible and manageable cluster of countries with similar issues and needs that can benefit from sharing of expertise, infrastructure, and programming).

Second, the notion of what a region is fundamentally about becomes challenging and potentially somewhat blurred as the different components of the role of a region can have very different drivers. We can identify at least five important components of the role of a region.

Specifically, the role could encompass the following:

- planning, management, and accountability
- shared technical expertise
- regional and multicountry programs
- donor relationships
- shared support functions and infrastructure

Each of these has somewhat different characteristics and drivers, with different implications for the optimum size for a region. This analysis has been summarized in table 1.1.

Having considered the various drivers in our analysis, we believe there is a strong argument for much smaller regions, perhaps including only two to five countries. There are a number of useful advantages to this approach. For example, it should help to

- bring together countries or mini-regions or zones with a more similar context, in terms of needs, culture, and even language (e.g., Uganda, Kenya, Tanzania)
- facilitate a stronger sense of sharing and mutual support, as well as form local working relationships to provide mutual assistance

Table 1.1
Components of the Regional Role of International NGOs

Component of Role	Characteristic	Optimum Size
1. Node of planning and management	Span of control important; location ideally close to countries supervised	Lends itself to large regions; for example, Africa or West Africa, implying ten to fifteen countries
2. Shared technical expertise	Needs to be close to field; experts who are contributing day to day at the field level	Lends itself to a very small cluster of countries (three to five) to be useful and accessible; expertise can be dispersed within country operations, though coordinated from one point
3. Regional and multicountry programs	Must be located at the natural hub of the mini-region, related to the center of political or economic influence	Located at the natural hub of the mini-region, related to the center of political or economic influence
4. Donor relationships	Needs to be aligned with the local nodes of the most strategic donors of the agency	Will depend on context and the donor
5. Shared support functions and infrastructure	Requires common context and language to be efficient	Lends itself to a smaller cluster of countries because of local complexities (two to five countries), probably managed from a single location

- share technical expertise, which could be hosted on a distributed basis in various country or field offices or in the most pragmatic location
- establish shared support functions and infrastructure, where feasible
- build stronger camaraderie and affinity across country program teams, which provides the opportunity to provide greater mutual

support and backup, for example, in the event of unexpected issues or in disaster situations and, finally, as a result of all of the above

- provide the opportunity for reducing the nonprogrammatic cost base in each individual program country

One country office could potentially act as a regional hub for the region, or aspects of the regional capacity can be housed in different locations across the region. Through this approach, INGOs can begin to achieve some of the local economies of scale to make them more efficient and robust local organizations and also begin to address the issue of the North–South imbalance that has been part of the legacy of many INGOs.

North–South Power Balance

Many large INGOs have an organizational construct that was devised in the *charity* era and is characterized by resources mainly collected in the richer North and distributed in the South. While a number are making notable efforts to evolve their organization and governance models, they may not be adapting at the pace and with as much conviction as one might hope to better align with up-to-date thinking on development good practice and particularly in relation to the desire for more "power equity" between the North and the South.

However, there are some signs of progress, for example, with the intent to establish more autonomous Southern affiliates for organizations such as ActionAid, World Vision, Plan International, Oxfam International, and others, particularly in emerging economies such as India, Indonesia, South Africa, and Brazil.

However, we feel that the "center of gravity" of senior management decision making is still too frequently locked in remote headquarters locations in the North. Some of the earlier recommendations (such as the concept of distributed or virtual headquarters, dispersed global leadership teams, and the evolution of modern matrix structural forms) should also provide a very substantive opportunity for meaningful inclusion of Southern affiliates and talent within a more balanced sense of power between the North and the South.

Appropriate Legal Structures

For those who bemoan the complexity of legal structures, with myriad separate legal entities including boards of directors in each country in the North and increasingly in the South, we feel the notion of dramatically simplifying the legal structures is not a silver bullet and not likely to happen any time soon. In fact, this complication will become greater as more and more program countries evolve to have their own formal legal structures, with greater local autonomy, albeit within more cohesive global organizations. Hence, the most practical response, we believe, is to live with this at least for now and to identify and implement some key requirements to make the totality of the organization work for maximum impact, irrespective of the legal constructs that exist.

As a parallel, in the corporate world most organizations manage to achieve a pragmatic separation of international management structures and processes on the one hand and legal structures on the other. The latter are typically designed to comply with tax and other legal obligations and are invisible to many of the staff and managers who look after day-to-day operations. There is little reason in our view why large INGOs could not take a similar approach. However, we recognize it will take strong, mature leadership and well-functioning planning, performance management, and accountability processes to achieve this.

Sensible Representative Governance

Finally, on legal structures and governance, the existence of a split governance structure is becoming more common and one that can work well, as long as the remit of both levels is explicit and contained. Large INGOs do need an international board, with a manageable number of people, say between eight and twelve, with the skills, expertise, credibility, and range of perspectives to guide and supervise the direction and performance of the overall agency on an ongoing basis. Practically, this cannot be fully representative of every entity of the organization North and South, but it should ideally be as representative as possible.

This board should meet quarterly or biannually to deal with issues of strategic importance, to ensure that financial and reputation matters are properly overseen, and to approve the overall strategy and global financial plans for the organization.

The board needs to be appointed by, and ultimately be accountable to, a representative oversight or supervisory board that meets much less frequently (probably no more often than every two or three years). This group should have the ultimate sign-off for major changes in strategic direction and should also ensure that the mission and the charter of the organization are protected and refined as needed.

1.5. Call to Action

The authors are not portraying these as either revolutionary requirements on the one hand or easy to implement on the other. Neither do we expect that readers will agree with all of our views or that all of our conclusions and recommendations will be appropriate for all INGOs. However, we hope that the shapes analysis and resultant recommendations can be provocative and instructive for large INGOs, igniting a serious debate on organizational glue and ensuring that they will, over the coming decades, continue to build on the considerable progress they have already made as major international players in the fight against poverty.

To conclude, we propose the following four actions:

1. Engage your leadership team to do a self-assessment on where your organization stands based on the recommendations and suggestions in section 1.4. Table 1.2 is a straightforward self-assessment template for executives of INGOs to plot where they feel their organizations are in respect to each of the core requirements and suggestions.

2. Carry out a rapid mapping of decision-making power against the detailed shapes template: where you were five years ago, where you are today, and where you feel you really need to be as an organization in five years. What are the areas that seem to spark the greatest debate among your leadership team?

3. Try to seek alignment within your leadership team on the most critical gaps or issues that need to be addressed.

4. If you agree you have some progress to make, seek to identify the most effective sequence to tackle the gaps you have identified, prioritizing no more than two or three for attention over the next eighteen months. It may help to do a rapid "causal loop" map to understand the interrelationship between the different aspects. This should help give you guidance on the most urgent aspects to tackle.

Notes

1. Marc Lindenberg and Coralie Bryant, *Going Global* (Bloomfield, CT: Kumarian Press, 2001).

2. M. Goold and A. Campbell, *Strategies and Styles: The Role of the Centre in Managing Diversified Corporations* (Oxford: Basil Blackwell, 1987).

Table 1.2
Self-Evaluation Template

Not Hopeful			Hopeful	
We are nowhere. There is no hope!	We have tried, but there are few signs of real progress.	Core Requirements	Some progress, though we are not there yet!	We are there!
		Program Legitimacy		
		1. Quality local programs with sustainable impact		
		2. Alignment around a "theory of change" and programmatic approach		
		3. Ruthless clarity and alignment on organizational core competencies (current and future)		
		4. Capacity, contribution, and impact on an international/global level		
		Operational Maturity		
		5. Mind-set of dual citizenship		
		6. Essential global processes aligned at a sensible level		
		7. Integrated organizational planning, performance, and accountability		
		Credible Leadership and Governance		
		8. Single, integrated global leadership team		
		9. Matrix management approach, aligned to management and process maturity		
		10. Minimal/virtual headquarters		
		11. Mini-regions with interlinked contexts and programs		
		12. North–South power balance		
		13. Appropriate legal structures		
		14. Sensible governance representation		

3. Accenture internal research, 1991.

4. Robert S. Kaplan and David P. Norton, *The Balanced Scorecard* (Boston, MA: Harvard Business School Press, 1996).

5. Robert S. Kaplan and David P. Norton, "The Balanced Scorecard: Measures That Drive Performance," *Harvard Business Review* (January–February 1992): 71–79.

2

Good at What?

The Core Competencies of International NGOs: What Are They? What Do They Need to Be?

Abstract

This chapter was written for the attention of senior executives, CEOs, chairs, and active board members of large international NGOs (INGOs) who are concerned about one of the biggest central questions facing large INGOs today: **In a world of dramatically changing context, what is the role of INGOs in the next decade?**

There are major changes afoot: ongoing shifts in thinking on effective development approaches; relentless calls for evidence of sustainable impact and value for money; changing roles and contributions from other stakeholders, including the private sector; the arrival of newer organizations who are duplicating the activities of traditional NGOs; and the emergence of many new areas of need. Add to this the transformational effect of new technological possibilities that make the world a much smaller, more integrated place. As almost every INGO increases its efforts to become better organized, more efficient, more coordinated internally, and more integrated externally, we need to address the $1 million question: What are large INGOs really good at? What are their core competencies today, and what do they need to be in the future? That's assuming that large INGOs have a useful role to play in the future.

In this chapter we refer back to the original thinking of C. K. Prahalad and Gary Hamel, published in the classic *Harvard Business Review* article "The Core Competence of the Corporation" (May–June 1990). The intention is to apply the same approach to INGOs and see what lessons and conclusions can be drawn. We identify a broad menu of core "generic" competencies for large INGOs. We explore how well NGOs line up today against these generic competence areas and also try to predict how their importance or relevance might change in the future.

We argue that the idea of core competencies, properly and deliberately thought through, can be a very productive way to help large INGOs achieve a more precise strategic focus. It can help INGOs clarify which capability investments are most important for the future and help spawn new innovative programs and products that are based on their core competence. It can also enable others to see more clearly where and when to partner with them and ultimately provide them with a credible source of comparative advantage into the future. We believe that the management debate around strategic focus, which is often articulated in terms of choices around geography or sectors, might more productively be conducted around core competencies. This is one of the key messages of this chapter.

2.1. Introduction

Why a Rethink? Why Now?

The idea of carrying out, from time to time, some considered reflection and examination of one's role, and hence what one needs to be really good at, seems to be a sensible step for any organization that wants to stay relevant. However, for large international development and relief agencies, in the midst of a dramatically changing environment, we believe that the need for some radical reflection is well overdue. Why? There are six fundamental factors that are particularly important in prompting some rethinking at this time.

1. First, there has, for some time, been an **ongoing shift in development thinking**. A good example of this is the recognition of the need to work more collaboratively, often in a supporting role, with a range of other stakeholders such as local government institutions, local community-based organizations, or local civil society organizations. Another related aspect of this is the shift in emphasis, with a focus less on the delivery of basic services to poor communities to more on a much more supportive role, helping local communities build their own capacity and become more aware of their basic legal rights, as well as the possibilities for their own social and economic progress.

2. There is an ever-increasing clamor for stronger **evidence of sustainable impact** from the programs supported and implemented by INGOs. Hence, as INGOs learn from more advanced monitoring and evaluation systems and gain a deeper understanding of the impact of different types of and approaches to program design and implementation, it is inevitable that they should review the scope of activities and programs they engage in, drawing back from more questionable areas and concentrating on areas where there is clearer evidence of lasting impact.

3. The role and **involvement of other major actors** affecting development has changed significantly over the past decade and is continuing to change. For example, the private sector is increasingly regarded as essential in driving sustainable economic development and as important to achieving sustainable poverty alleviation. The private sector is becoming much more active from a number of angles. Many companies have come to appreciate that developing countries are strategically important to their future business success, be it in accessing new customers and markets, sourcing raw materials, or tapping into new investment opportunities.

4. There is a range of **new organizations, either not for profits, for profits, or hybrids**, that are providing the types of services that INGOs saw as their sole territory in the past. Examples include companies such as Chemonics International, Blackwater, The Louis Berger Group, Kiva, and Development

Alternatives, as well as in some more well-known names such as PwC and BearingPoint.

5. There is a growing need for INGOs to contribute to some **new areas in need of attention**, such as issues relating to the impact of climate change in developing countries. Another example is the area of regional and international advocacy in an interconnected world. There is an increasing opportunity, in fact obligation, for some INGOs to participate much more seriously as contributors in relation to international policy, as well as in the implementation of international policy at national and international levels.

6. Last, and by no means least, in a world of ever-increasing connectivity facilitated by **waves of new technological possibilities**, particularly information technology, the context for the work of large INGOs is changing significantly. In the old world, the INGO often acted as an intermediary between the richer North and the less fortunate South. With new and emerging technology possibilities, INGOs need to ensure that they are a value-adding facilitator. Moreover, it is critical that large established INGOs do not invest large sums to automate a model of operation for a role and associated set of competencies that may rapidly become outdated.

Hence, we believe the time is right for INGOs to revisit their role and contributions and clarify the core competencies that they nurture and build if they wish to maximize their contribution in a changing and more interconnected environment. This is particularly relevant for INGOs when they undertake strategic planning reviews and should be a standard part of any such exercise.

2.2. The Idea of Core Competencies: Revisiting the Original Concept

Do you remember the brand name of your first TV? I certainly do. Our rental TV was the center of the local community at a time when televisions were still relatively scarce. Our first was a PYE, though I also remember names like Pilot, Bush, GEC, and Thompson. In those days, TVs broke down a lot, and we frequently had to get ours swapped over for another that worked (though often not for long). Whatever happened to these famous household names of the 1960s and 1970s?

We came across some of these names again in the classic *Harvard Business Review* article by C. K. Prahalad and Gary Hamel, "The Core Competence of the Corporation,"[1] originally released in June 1990. In our research for this book, we were curious to see whether the ideas from this seminal piece of business literature could be helpful in understanding more deeply what INGOs are really good at or should be focusing their attention on, particularly at an organization-wide level. In doing this we had a number of fairly straightforward questions, for example:

- What are the one or two real core competencies of a typical international development or humanitarian NGO today?
- Which competencies are weak or need strengthening?
- Which competencies have growing relevance? Or have declining relevance?
- What new competencies are needed to meet the challenges of a new and changing world? Are these being identified and nurtured?

With regard to those household names of the 1960s and 1970s, it is interesting to refer to the summary extract from Prahalad and Hamel's *Harvard Business Review* article in relation to the color television market.

Example: TV Market in 1970s and 1980s

In the 1970s and 1980s, many American and European companies—like GE, Motorola, GTE, Thorn and GEC—chose to exit the colour television business which they regarded as mature. If by "mature" they meant that they had run out of new product ideas at precisely the moment global rivals had targeted the TV business for entry, then yes, the industry was mature. But it certainly wasn't mature in the sense that all opportunities to enhance and apply video-based competencies had been exhausted. In ridding themselves of their television businesses . . . they closed the door on a whole stream of future opportunities reliant on video-based competencies.

Source. Prahalad and Hamel, "The Core Competence of the Corporation," pp. 84–85.

Why is this relevant? One of the central arguments on core competencies in this chapter is that organizations that think only in terms of discrete end products and end markets, and manage and invest on this basis, sacrifice the long-term success at the expense of shortsighted gains. In the TV market, organizations that saw their business with a longer-term lens, investing, growing, and exploiting their core competencies, arrived at a different set of conclusions. Instead of seeing the color TV market as a mature, slow-growing market, they saw the beginning of a new wave of opportunities that allowed them to replace the old household names with names such as Sony, Phillips, Sanyo, and Panasonic, all of which remain thriving businesses today.

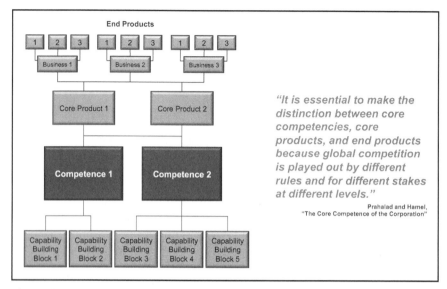

Figure 2.1 The roots of competitiveness.

These new players had a relentless long-term focus, with a portfolio of strategic investments across the totality of the corporation, as well as a plethora of strategic alliances to secure and strengthen critical capability building blocks in support of their target set of core competencies.

Over a period of less than one decade, not only did they replace the old household names in the television market, but they also took over and dominated a whole set of other new and emerging markets because of their focus on core competencies, which they saw as the primary platform of their business success.

What did Prahalad and Hamel actually mean by core competence? They describe the idea of visualizing core competencies in terms of a large tree, which is appealing in understanding how the core competence fits with core products and end products (see figure 2.1). This is a very helpful framework to understand the interrelationship between different levels of the tree and how productive energy can flow through the tree from its roots to deliver sustained organizational success. It particularly shows us how energy needs to be invested at different levels to create a successful business in the short and longer term and that core competencies are at the heart of the process.

Core competencies are supported by a range of underlying capability building blocks, which are hard to develop, and frequently organizations need to look to focused investments, strategic alliances, or specially targeted acquisitions to expedite what might otherwise be a very long process. It is helpful to be able to articulate a small number of core competencies (say two or three) to provide focus and clarity as to what the organization is really about. These are **typically built up over a period of five, ten, or even twenty years.**

What Do We Really Mean by Core Competencies?

Core competence is deep commitment to working across organizations' boundaries.

Core competencies are the collective learning in the organization, especially how to coordinate diverse production skills and integrate multiple streams of technologies.

Unlike many assets, core competencies are enhanced as they are applied and shared, but competencies still need to be nurtured and protected; knowledge fades if it is not used.

In the short run, a company's competitiveness derives from the price performance attributes from its current products. However, over time all survivors converge on similar and formidable standards of cost and quality.

In the long run, competitiveness derives from an ability to build, at lower cost, and more speedily than competitors, the core competencies that spawn improved and unanticipated products.

There are many companies that have had the potential to build core competencies but failed to do so because top management was unable to conceive of the company as anything other than a collection of discrete businesses.

By focusing on core competencies, Canon has given us personal copiers; Honda has moved from motorcycles to four-wheel off-road buggies. Sony developed the 8mm camcorder, Yamaha the digital piano.

Honda's core competence in engines and power trains gave it a distinctive advantage in car, motorcycle, lawn mower, and generator businesses. Chrysler, unlike Honda, saw engines and power trains as one more component and soon became dependent on Mitsubishi and Hyundai, and began a long period of competitive decline.

NEC's strategic intent in linking computing and communications and components believed there would be enormous opportunities for any company that had developed the competencies to serve all three markets.

Casio must harmonize know-how in miniaturization, microprocessor design, material science, and ultra-thin precision casing—the same skills as it needs to produce miniature card calculators, pocket TVs, and digital watches.

Source. Prahalad and Hamel, "The Core Competence of the Corporation," pp. 79–86.

Prahalad and Hamel argued that the focus on core competencies is essential for long-term competitiveness. It needs to be **viewed at a corporate level, looking beyond the boundaries of traditional business unit thinking** that has become a strong focus of management decision making in many traditional organizations. They identified a range of great examples in their article, including companies such as Sony, Phillips, Canon, NEC, Casio, 3M, Honda, and Yamaha, all of which are still thriving organizations today. As Prahalad and Hamel emphasized, "In the race for global dominance, these companies built global brand umbrellas by proliferating products out of their core competencies" (p. 86).

2.3. Core Competencies of International NGOs

So how does this translate to large INGOs? We were prompted to reflect on this on hearing some comments from a senior NGO executive recently who cited that "child sponsorship" was a mature and potentially declining product. At around the same time, we heard a similar remark in relation to "international volunteering." Is this really true? Or is this perspective akin to GTE's view of the television market it exited in the 1980s and 1990s, or Chrysler's remarks on car engines when they built up a reliance on engines from their competitors?

We looked at a range of INGOs, trying to analyze and delineate their core competencies, core products, and end products. We found this to be feasible and also very helpful. We also tried to isolate the underlying capabilities or subcompetencies that underpin each of the core competencies.

While we were carrying out the analysis, an interesting linkage emerged between different levels, for example, between core products on the one hand and core competencies on the other. Is child sponsorship a core competence, a core product, or just an end product? We concluded that it is best described as a core product, though one that has enabled a number of organizations to develop specific competencies and underpinning capabilities over several decades of experience. This provides something that is difficult to replicate but needs to be refined and nurtured to remain of real value for the future as technology possibilities, development understanding, and donor and consumer behavior and expectations evolve. How does one define this competence and its underlying capabilities? Once we can define and understand it, how can it be used to spawn new and evolving product opportunities over time?

Having completed our assessment, we concluded that the idea of core competencies can be very powerful and help INGOs reflect on what they are really good at and what they need to get good at to be able to spawn the range of products and programs that will allow them to continue to grow their impact. However, as indicated in the original *Harvard Business Review* article, the definition of what constitutes a core competence is not an exact science, and one should not get overly pedantic. What is merely a capability for one NGO may well be a core competence for another.

Illustrative Generic Core Competence Menu for INGOs

Table 2.1 sets out one generic spectrum or menu of core competencies that we believe are relevant to development and humanitarian agencies. For ease, we grouped the competencies into three categorizations:

Table 2.1
Illustrative Core Competence Generic Menu for International NGOs

Expediting the human and economic development process	1. Helping **build capacity** of local community-based organizations and district and state institutions
	2. Building awareness of rights and responsibilities and addressing **injustice and human rights violations**
	3. Mobilizing local, national, and **international attention and progress** on specific development blockages
	4. **Bridging different sectors** to achieve development progress at local, national, and international levels within communities, government, business and private sectors, and the international political landscape
	5. **Connecting people** in different communities, sectors, countries, and markets to achieve sustainable development progress
	6. Stimulating a sense of **hope and progress** for people and communities in poverty
	7. Helping **initiate and mobilize critical infrastructure projects** (roads, ports, dams, telecoms, infrastructure)
Mitigating the effects of disasters	8. Delivering **fast, effective humanitarian response** for natural disaster or conflicts
	9. Providing preemergency preparation to help communities and countries in poverty **reduce the impact of potential disasters**
Basic service delivery	10. Delivering **essential services** where there is deep systemic failure

- Expediting the human and economic development process in poor countries;
- Mitigating the effects of disasters (natural or man-made); and
- Delivering basic services in cases where there is deep systemic failure.

This list of competencies is merely intended as a generic, cumulative set for illustrative purposes. The real insight comes from the particular definition of core competence that is specific and potentially unique to an individual organization given its history, strengths, and strategic direction.

In this respect, we have been very taken with and impressed by the specific focus of AMREF, which has isolated "connecting the formal and informal health systems in Africa" as one of its key areas of focus. This innovative definition of core competence is founded on the history and the strengths of the organization and provides a very clear focus for much of AMREF's work and investment for the future.

Another very good example is VSO, which in its new global strategy describes its single core competence as "bringing people together to fight poverty."[2] The clarity and alignment provides a very clear mandate to significantly scale certain activities and programs, for example, South–South volunteering, national volunteering, and its youth exchange program. Equally important for VSO, this newfound clarity is helping to establish a very clear rationale to say no to inappropriate activities, promoted by other organizations, for example, around opportunities sometimes referred to as "volunt-tourism."

Using the Idea of Core Competence

The real crunch comes when one begins to explore, for any particular INGO, what an organization is doing to understand and nurture core competencies at an organization-wide level:

- How much board and senior management time is spent on appraising and challenging the essential role and contribution of each INGO in light of a rapidly changing development context?
- How much senior management attention, at an international level, is devoted to exploiting the full competencies that have been developed over several decades?

- How much senior management attention, at an international level, is spent on strengthening these competencies for the longer term?
- How well does management appreciate the critical underpinning capabilities that nurture and develop competencies for the future and ensure that these are protected and grown? Possible examples of this are the work required to analyze, in detail, the root causes of poverty in any given context or the design of detailed program proposals and plans. This could be regarded as a critical underpinning capability that supports most, if not all, of the core competencies in our illustrative menu. How often do INGOs outsource this role to external consultants, reducing the opportunity for building cumulative learning for the future?

We feel that insufficient time is really devoted to these fundamental questions. This is reducing the chance that the whole will indeed be greater than the sum of the parts or at least as great as it could potentially be.

To help support this type of analysis, figure 2.2 lays out a segregation of core competencies, indicative core products that feed from these core competencies, and some underlying capabilities that nurture these competencies. This is not intended to be a "right answer" by any means, but merely a way of prompting the thought process that may be productive for large INGOs when considering how to make the whole greater than the sum of the individual parts.

Most INGOs will be well served by focusing on one or two core competencies at an organization-wide level in order to establish a real differentiated position in the minds of those whom they are trying to support, as well as in minds of major donors. The observation that could be made for a number of major INGOs is that they attempt to operate as if they possess most, if not all, of the core competencies mentioned above. We feel this is not a good recipe for maximizing their long-term contribution in an ever-evolving sector.

Relative Strengths and Future Relevance

How has the importance of these competencies changed over time? Can we assess the typical strength of these competencies in the profile of INGOs? Figure 2.3 describes a simplified and averaged view of the relative strength of the menu of core competencies we identified. This also indicates a perspective on which of these core competencies are going to become even more central if INGOs are to achieve their mission over the next ten to fifteen years.

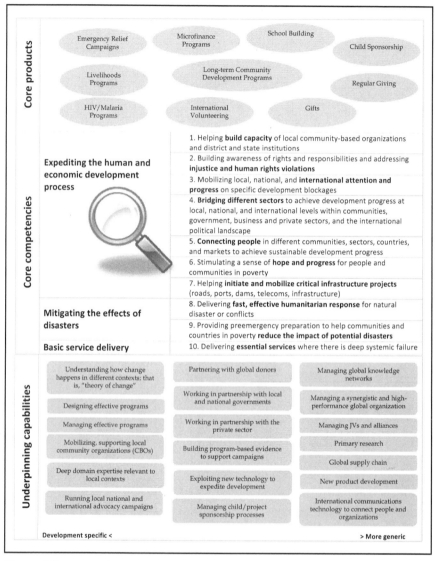

Figure 2.2 Core products, core competencies, and underpinning capabilities.

2.4. Conclusions and Implications

The following is a summary of the six main conclusions from our analysis.

1. **Clarity on organization-wide core competencies is a useful concept to help with management focus in the near term and sustainability in the**

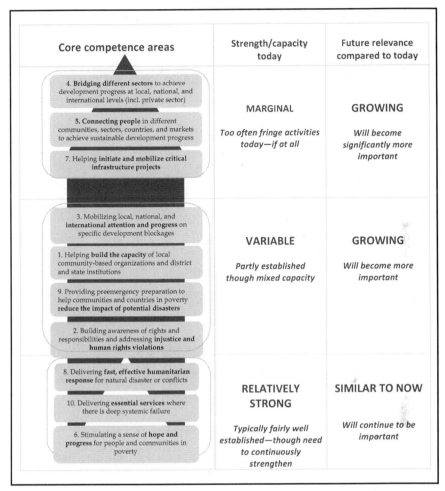

Figure 2.3 Assessment of core competence, relative strengths, and future relevance.

longer term. We believe that one of the most important roles of the global organization is to foster and invest in core competencies that are required for future longer-term success. Like commercial organizations, INGOs that become exclusively fixated on short-term product, program, or business unit performance are likely to miss out on the opportunity to stay relevant and deliver a sustainable, long-term contribution. Clarity of and focus on a few core competencies can be a useful glue to bind the organization together, helping it to deliver more than the sum of the parts. Don't confuse your current products and interventions with your core competencies.

NGOs need to examine what their current competencies are and how they need to evolve and be strengthened to be relevant in light of major trends and changes in the environment in which they operate. This is not an easy task. It requires considerable thought, discussion, and iteration. Real clarity and alignment takes considerable brainpower and effort. This is also likely to help management see, with greater precision, those activities and programs the organization would be well suited to participate in, as well as those opportunities to leave to others.

2. **Most INGOs are too widely spread and do not have a realistic chance of gaining real depth in all of the core competencies implicitly implied by their strategies.** Many large INGOs are explicitly or implicitly trying to establish competencies in a very wide set of geographies (often across 50 to 100 countries) and seeking to address multiple sector domains (e.g., health, education, etc.). This is likely to result in at least two important challenges and risks. First, because they lack sufficient focus, it is unlikely that they will be able to develop the necessary depth of competencies to be able to deliver high-quality programs and impact across their entire portfolio of activities. Second, as a number of INGOs expand and evolve their activities to a point that they all cover the same territory, it will be impossible to achieve a distinctive position in the minds of donors and other important external stakeholders. One implication of this is that if mistakes or failures occur at a particular point of an organization, the reputation of the entire organization will suffer and most probably also will the reputation of other INGOs, who are seen as broadly equivalent (sometimes referred to as Gresham's law).

We believe that the management debate around strategic focus, which is often articulated in terms of choices around geography or sector domains, might be more productively conducted around core competencies. This is one of the key findings of this chapter.

3. **Alignment on your contribution to development is likely to be an essential foundation stone in defining your core competencies.** Getting alignment on core competencies is likely to be challenging if the broader leadership of the INGO is not well aligned on the organization's specific contribution to the development process. At least at an implicit level this is helped by clarity and alignment on how change happens in poor communities and countries, which is sometimes referred to as a *theory of change*. This could be manifested, for example, in agreement on what a good development program looks like in practice. If there is obvious dissent between different parts of the organization in this regard, it is highly unlikely you will be productive in nurturing your selected core competencies for the future.

4. **Strengthening and evolving carefully selected core competencies requires sustained and aligned efforts across all parts of the organization.** Core competencies that give real sustainability and differentiation are likely to have a number of underpinning building blocks or capabilities that need to be built and strengthened one by one, over an extended period of time (e.g., five, ten, or fifteen years) across multiple nodes of the organization. This requires disciplined analysis and planning of the underlying capabilities that nurture competencies for the long haul. Efforts to strengthen core competencies need to permeate all parts of the organization: spanning program and funding entities, lines of business, regional offices, and headquarters.

5. **Use newfound clarity on your core competencies to spawn and mainstream new products.** Once clear on your core competencies, enter into creative debate on how these core competencies can translate to successful new programs or products. This can be a very useful way of driving innovative development of your product/program portfolio. For example, VSO's newfound clarity on the core competence of "bringing people together to fight poverty"[3] gave it a much clearer mandate to launch and scale up new innovative product areas to complement the international volunteering product.

6. **Alliances and joint ventures, as well as mergers, can supplement or speed up acquisition of missing (or weak) core competencies.** Just like organizations in the commercial world, INGOs can be creative to speed up the process of acquiring and strengthening core competencies for the future. This might involve joint ventures and alliances, which is a classical approach in the commercial world. This can reduce the cost and speed up the process, which otherwise could take far too long.

To conclude, we would like to encourage NGO executives to reflect critically on how the idea of core competence maps onto their particular organizations. Table 2.2 is intended as an aid to begin such a reflection process.

Notes

1. C. K. Prahalad and Gary Hamel, "The Core Competence of the Corporation," *Harvard Business Review* (May–June 1990): 79–90.

2. http://www.vsointernational.org/vso-today/how-we-do-it/our-strategy.asp.

3. http://www.vsointernational.org/vso-today/how-we-do-it/our-strategy.asp.

Table 2.2
Self-Assessment Template

How strong is your competence today?	Core competence areas (generic framework)			
	Expediting the human and economic development process			
	Helping build capacity of local community-based organizations and district and state institutions	Building awareness of rights and responsibilities and addressing injustice and human rights violations	Mobilizing local, national, and international attention and progress on specific development blockages	Bridging different sectors to achieve development progress at local, national, and international levels
A. World class—A leader				
B. Better than the rest—though space for improvement				
C. Similar to best of the rest				
D. Average for the sector				
E. Below average for the sector				
F. Fringe competence				
G. Pretty nonexistent				

Table 2.2
(continued)

Core competence areas (generic framework)					
Expediting the human and economic development process			Mitigating the effects of disasters		Basic service delivery
Connecting people in different communities, sectors, countries, and markets to achieve sustainable development progress	Stimulating a sense of **hope** **and progress** for people and communities in poverty	Helping **initiate and** **mobilize** **critical** **infrastructure** **projects** (roads, ports, dams, telecoms, infrastructure)	Delivering **fast, effective** **humanitarian** **response** for natural disaster or conflicts	Providing preemergency preparation to help communities and countries in poverty **reduce the** **impact of** **potential** **disasters**	Delivering **essential** **services** where there is deep systemic failure

Evolving Structures
of International NGOs

Is There a Right Answer?

Abstract

This chapter was written for the attention of senior executives, CEOs, and active board members of large international NGOs (INGOs). It is intended to provoke, challenge, and generate new ideas on the topic of **the best structural forms for such organizations.** While there is much literature in this space for private sector organizations, there is little recent material for the development sector. This chapter seeks to leverage existing private sector thinking for the benefit of INGOs.

We begin this chapter with a short historical review of the evolution of global thinking on organizational structural forms in the private sector, tracking the ongoing quest for high performance, improved quality, better customer service, and lower costs. We also reflect on the efforts "beyond structure" that resulted when practitioners and academics recognized that structure was but one of a number of ingredients that contributed to creating a more effective and efficient international organization.

We then review equivalent developments and progress in the international development and relief sector. There has been considerable growth over the past decade. This growth has also been matched by impressive progress in terms of understanding and strengthening development approaches and interventions. However, despite some very encouraging progress in a variety of areas, it is our conclusion that the evolution of structures and associated management techniques at an international level has lagged behind what can be observed in the private sector.

We explore some of the particular factors that we feel need to be taken into account in the consideration of structure in this sector. This chapter outlines a range of structural variants for INGOs and explores the main characteristics of these structures, the associated pros and cons, and their appropriateness in different situations. We argue that while there is no single correct organizational structure for all, the simple (predominantly geographical-based) structure that is still frequently adopted by large INGOs is no longer equipped to cope with the nature, scope, and scale of today's needs.

We go on to address the issue of managing structural change for INGOs. In particular, we look at how to synchronize a range of factors that need to be progressed in concert to ensure that any structural form has a fair chance of success. We also explore the concept of "organizational glue," which comprises "motivating" and "enabling" glue, and argue that understanding these two types of glue is critical to navigate serious organizational change, and especially so for organizations in this sector.

3.1. Historical Overview of Global Thinking on Organizational Structure

What Is Structure For?

Organizational structure is a much discussed topic, it is easy to debate, and it is tangible to most within any large organization. What do we actually mean by structure? At its simplest level, structure provides a degree of order in the use of resources, people, and money. It is often linked to the specification of roles and responsibilities and helps define the formal relationships between staff: "I am responsible for X, I work closely with Y, and we all report to Z." It signifies power and decision-making rights. It also provides the glue that helps bind or unite the efforts of everyone in the organization toward the delivery of a common mission.

It is a dimension of an organization that can be changed quickly, with effects that can be seen immediately for those it impacts. It is easier, and perceptibly cheaper, to change than systems, processes, capacity, or behavior. And it is an alluring temptation to new CEOs, who see it as a way of tackling the ills of an organization, demonstrating that a new broom can sweep clean, bringing rapid change and improvements. It is so tempting to tinker.

Evolving Thinking on Structure Over the Past Century

Debate on organizational structures and models has continued in endless waves ever since the revolutionary thinking of Frederick Taylor[1] a century ago. Taylor argued that higher performance could be achieved by simplification and specialization, that is, by breaking tasks down into their smallest components and allowing distinct groups of workers to become specialists at each step of a process. Hence, he proposed, organizational structures should be designed to manage the structured flow of standardized tasks. To maximize the productivity of the teams on each task, the variation in range of products should be kept to an absolute minimum. Henry Ford, head of the Ford Motor Company in the 1920s, epitomized this emphasis on standardization with his now famous quote in relation to the Ford Model T: "Any customer can have a car painted any color that he wants so long as it is black."[2]

The organizational construct that emerged from that period is often loosely referred to as a "bureaucracy," implying that there are clear formal descriptions of roles and relationships, an extensive rule book and set of procedures, and clear measurement of discrete outputs at each stage of the production process. This approach discouraged the individual worker on the factory floor from using his or her discretion.

Table 3.1

Summary of Henry Mintzberg's Five Configurations of Internal Structure (1979)

Organizational Form	Characteristics	Coordinating Mechanism	Good For
Simple structure	Little or no technology structure, few support staff, a loose division of labor, low specialization, and a small managerial hierarchy operating in an organic fashion	Direct supervision, with a hierarchical form of control; important decisions are handled centrally; and the strategic apex, typically one or two people, is the dominant part of the organization	Typically used in the early years of an organization or for small organizations in simple though dynamic environments
Machine bureaucracy	Rules and regulations, formal communications, and hierarchical chains of authority and decision making; large technology structure, provides the analysts who standardize the operators' work within clear parameters	Standardization of work; strong technological and administrative forms of control predominate	Very large organization producing standard outputs in a stable environment
Professional bureaucracy	Professionals in the operating core control their own work of diagnosis and problem solving	Standardization of skills and methodology, as well as peer work control	Environments requiring a complex knowledge base, though environments are relatively stable
Divisionalized structure	Communication between HQ and divisions highly formalized; midlevel hierarchy has considerable autonomy for managing its own division; each division is typically a machine bureaucracy	Control of standard outputs at a higher level, for example, revenue or profit	Where a very large organization has reached maturity point in several different product markets
Adhocracy	Support staff are the dominant group, and structure is characterized by everything that is organic rather than mechanistic; innovation and change rather than stability are central	Mutual adjustment and control exercised in person and in an unobtrusive manner	Suitable for complex, dynamic, disparate environments or early stages of an organization's life

Source. H. Mintzberg, *The Structuring of Organizations* (Englewood Cliffs, NJ: Prentice Hall, 1979).

The debate evolved through the decades as companies sought new and incremental ways of organizing to drive higher productivity, reduce unit costs, and improve quality. The thinking on organizational forms was moved forward to its next major iteration by the contributions of contingency theorists such as Galbraith and Mintzberg.[3] The latter became famous for his characterization of the five-structure configurations that are still referred to today in management literature. Each one is designed to deal with different sets of contingent factors (see table 3.1).

In summary, Mintzberg's five forms[4] are as follows:

1. **Simple structure** for newly formed organizations or small organizations in dynamic environments with a narrow product range.
2. **Machine bureaucracy** for large organizations in a stable environment where tasks and outputs can be standardized.
3. **Professional bureaucracy** for large organizations in a relatively stable though more complex environment where skills and methods (rather than tasks) can be standardized.
4. **Divisionalized structure** for very large organizations where multiple businesses have reached maturity in very different markets or sectors.
5. **Adhocracy** for organizations in complex, dynamic environments, where innovation and flexibility is important.

The simple principle that emerged at this time was that there was no right or wrong answer in terms of structural form; the challenge was to match the best structural form with the organizational needs and market context at any particular time.

Beyond Structure

Though the fascination with structural alternatives continued at a relentless pace in the 1970s, 1980s, and 1990s, the quest for higher performance progressed on a wider front than structure alone, with layers and layers of new ideas, models, and innovations, many originating from the United States and particularly from Japan. The new approaches such as "total quality," "continuous improvement," "six sigma," and "process reengineering" all took root at this time. Other important concepts were put forward by business academics such as Michael Porter with his ideas on "competitive advantage,"[5] Hamel and Prahalad with their insight into "core competence,"[6] and Peters and Waterman through their research in the popular book *In Search of Excellence*.[7] The debate also encompassed evolving thinking on leadership. A good example of this is the work of Jim Collins, particularly through the widely acclaimed book *Good to Great*.[8]

By this time, it was fully acknowledged that structure was just one of a number of factors contributing to strong organizational performance. Other dimensions such as strategy, skills and behaviors, processes and systems, and management and leadership capacity were also regarded as equally important ingredients for success. **In the private sector, it was common for organizations to experiment, testing new ideas and approaches in the quest to achieve improved comparative performance. It is fair to say that these new ideas, stimulated by the arrival of groundbreaking new technological possibilities, transformed the levels of productivity, quality, and innovation, as well as customer focus, over these decades.**

Evolution of the Matrix Structures

Returning to evolving thinking around structure, the idea of matrix structures, which was one manifestation of the adhocracy form from Mintzberg, had already been spawned in the 1960s to address the need to ensure both horizontal coordination and vertical flows of information.

Up to this point, workers at an operational level were organized either according to function or by product or market. Where high standards of work are required, particularly in smaller organizations working in a narrow product field, a purely functional-type structure seemed most appropriate. However, where a focus on customer markets was important and where the enterprise had several diversified product categories or geographical areas to serve or used a wide variety of different technologies, the product or market groupings had a lot of attraction. However, this left the question as to the best approach for fostering technical excellence while also satisfying customer needs in a responsive and holistic way.

In a fascinating account of the development of matrix structures in the US aerospace industry in 1973, Kingdon[9] describes how people had been content with functionally based technical excellence until the newly elected President Kennedy publicly promised to have a man on the moon by 1970, and time became of the essence. This made top National Aeronautics and Space Administration (NASA) management responsible for simultaneous delivery of a hugely complex multicomponent and multidisciplinary project that reached across the domains of government, highly specialized private contractors, and research organizations. At the same time, members of the Senate and Congress, as well as American taxpayers, wanted to see evidence of value for money. For NASA to get the best out of both product and functional worlds, it developed the concept of matrix structure. In addition, those responsible for procuring components or services for the space program looked for evidence from their suppliers and subcontractors that they were also similarly organized.

In matrix structures, specialists retain membership of a functional group with some allegiance to their specialist manager, while also being dedicated to a product or design team. Placed in the tricky position of answering to two bosses, members of these structures often find themselves in somewhat uncomfortable places. In the early days, this structure was seen as expensive to maintain and criticized for lack of clear accountability.

However, variants of matrix structures became popular across many industries in the private sector and also in realms of government and social service agencies. The extent and speed with which this new organization form has been adopted is testimony to the persuasiveness and inherent validity of this contingency approach. After much debate, and criticism, particularly in the 1980s, some form of matrix structure has become the norm in most large international corporations.

Today, many organizations have become comfortable with matrix structures, with a number of dimensions all formally represented in the management process. These dimensions can include functional expertise, as well as product, customer, geography, and asset groupings, to name just a few. Planning and management processes have evolved to facilitate the balancing of perspectives from different dimensions in both planning and day-to-day management processes. Human resource management is an important mechanism to positively encourage the right mind-set in staff working in a matrix structure.

3.2. Evolution of Structures of International NGOs

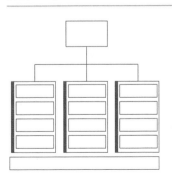

INGOs work in challenging, unstable, and demanding environments, implementing a very wide and dynamic range of programs and interventions. They have, arguably, progressed considerably in terms of their thinking in relation to the development process. They have improved their ability to understand local context, be it social, cultural, economic, or political. And though it is still an imperfect science, they are much more sophisticated in terms of selecting, designing, and implementing interventions at local, national, and international levels that have the best chance of delivering lasting positive results for any specific context. However, how have these agencies progressed internally in terms of the evolution of their organizational structures and associated techniques to improve performance and impact?

Structure in Context for International NGOs

In common with many organizations that grew from humble grassroots beginnings, NGO agencies typically started with a fairly simple structure. Units were defined around geographical boundaries, often based on field program units in developing countries, and often funded by a single funding office in the developed world.

Over time, as the scale of operations increased, these field units were grouped together to create country programs under the control of a country director. This approach provided the opportunity to establish functional specialization, initially in the areas of human resources, finance, and IT but also for key technical program areas such as health, HIV, agriculture, water, and gender. Hence, at a country level, the idea of a matrix structural form is not so unusual, with strong functional groups of specialists working in tandem with local community program managers to achieve the goals defined within their country's strategic plan.

As the number of country programs multiplied, regions were established, and regional directors were appointed to provide a layer of management to supervise and coordinate groups of country programs.

The management process that accompanied this form of structure was often established on a fairly basic, line of sight, relational style of management, with minimal processes and IT systems. Management process tended to be based on regular face-to-face visits, supplemented by program audits and a small number of basic reporting metrics. One of these might be around spend rates for committed program funding. Spending your money within the planned time period was regarded as good; not spending your planned allocation was bad. Though not always, this approach also tended to be related to a model of development sometimes referred to as the "resource transfer model" where money was raised in the affluent North and transferred to the poorer South for delivery of services and programs in areas of urgent need.

This sort of structure and management approach is to be expected for younger, smaller organizations, usually with a fairly simple range of program activities. And it is not unique to agencies in the development and relief sectors; it is, in fact, to be expected for most organizations in their formative years.

However, we believe that the persistence of this type of simplified model is now out of sync with the nature, scope, and scale of the challenges faced by many large international agencies today.

Programs are more complex and span many domains, such as health, education, agriculture, microfinance, and more. In addition to service delivery, INGOs are also increasingly engaging in "softer" work around empowerment, facilitation, capacity building, and governance. They employ a broader range of interventions and invest considerably more of their resources in advocacy and awareness activities at local, national, and international levels. They also work with large and increasingly sophisticated donors and partners. Finally, these international agencies are aligning themselves and integrating their efforts more closely with other government, civil society, and private sector organizations.

How have their organizational structures and management systems evolved to keep pace with this shift in variety, scope, scale, and sophistication of their activities? The short answer is that they have not!

INGOs' evolution to more sophisticated and appropriate organizational structures and management models have not kept pace with the evolution of their core activities.

Many agencies have been victims of their own success. Their impressive growth over the past decade has made it difficult to keep organizational capacity and sophistication in sync with the ever-growing scale of income and programs being managed. In part, these agencies are also impeded by complex international governance structures. Multiple boards and reporting relationships at national and international levels can sometimes be an impediment to decision-making and organization-strengthening initiatives.

The internal structures of some large INGOs have not materially changed significantly over the years, though some (e.g., World Vision International, Save the Children, and Care International, to name a few) are in the process of significantly refining, simplifying, and strengthening their global organizations.

Some are busily addressing duplication within their broader organizations by establishing a unified presence in all their program countries and, in some cases, defining a single international program structure to supervise the delivery of all programs globally. This should assist in minimizing duplication of management nodes and help eliminate unnecessary cost. It should also increase the opportunity to share best practice across countries and establish a more consistent philosophy and approach to program design and execution. Another benefit is that it will allow INGOs to interface more smoothly with partners and present a more coherent and compelling face to large donors.

For those who already enjoy a unitary program structure, many still have a "simple geographical structure," with a number of regional nodes of management coordinating local country programs, which are the key program units. However, in many cases, the role of country director is often regarded as the "best job" in an agency because it provides a reasonably high degree of control and a strong degree of local autonomy.

If you look across the operations of some large INGOs, the critic might argue that development programs are, in reality, a collection of "cottage businesses" wrapped in a thin veneer of an integrated global organization. Standing back, many of the new ideas and breakthroughs that we have observed in the private sector over the past decades have, by and large, been absent in the management of large INGOs.

Making Regions Work

Regional levels of coordination and management within INGOs seem to present a number of challenges that deserve comment. Too often, regional levels of management fail to operate effectively, sometimes being caught in the middle between a powerful headquarters and independent-minded country offices that have significant flexibility and autonomy. When we look at regional nodes more closely, we can observe that they are expected to play a number of roles that place different and sometimes conflicting demands on them. For example, they can be

- nodes of line management
- coordinators or providers of support functions (e.g., finance, HR)
- centers for shared technical expertise across program countries
- managers of pan-country programs where they exist
- liaison points with regional donors

The issue of regional management and coordination is discussed more fully in chapter 1, "Getting in Shape." However, these challenges are, in our view, a symptom of the limitations of the simple geographical structure with an overemphasis on a relationship style of management and which is not in tune with the needs of international agencies when they become larger and engaged in a more complex portfolio of activities.

Specific Factors or Peculiarities That Influence the Choice of Structure for Large International Agencies

When discussing innovations and improvements in the structures of large international agencies, we think it is important to take into account a number of attributes that are specific to these organizations.

1. **The geographic scope and number of domains across which these agencies typically stretch are enormous** in comparison to the modest size of their overall budgets and resources. These organizations are, arguably, spread far too thinly and cannot afford the desirable investment in coordinating mechanisms and structures that the scope of activities and geography might imply. Unsurprisingly, there has been a lack of historic investment in international enabling processes such as finance, human resources, and information technology, not to mention learning and knowledge management.

2. In addition to the issue of scope, a related challenge is the preferred mode of working. **A considerable proportion of INGO programs are implemented either partly or fully through partners.** While this is very desirable and laudable, it has important considerations for the way day-to-day activities need to be organized and managed.

3. There is a **natural tension between the need for local responsiveness on the one hand and an increasing need for international coordination and integration on the other.** Agencies need to be careful and flexible in the design of local programs to ensure that they are in tune with the local social, economic, and political contexts that they are trying to support. But they also need to be able to share best practices, align to the organizations' global strategy, follow global policies and methodologies, and coherently interface with global donors. This tension puts a particular strain on any international structural model.

4. There can sometimes be a **disconnect between stakeholders who provide the funding for programs, often based in the richer North, and the needs of beneficiaries** whom the agency is there to serve. NGO staff in the field have a strong sense of what interventions and support are most likely to result in the best sustainable impact on the ground. However, their views are sometimes not aligned with the understanding of donors, large and small, whose money is enormously valued but whose views and level of understanding can be variable. It should be noted, however, that with the increasing emergence of more enlightened international donor institutions with a growing presence in developing countries, this gap in understanding is slowly improving. A specific example of this is the considerable advance in understanding among leaders in the business community who are increasingly seeing developing countries as integral to their longer-term business growth and success.

5. The **complex set of board structures** that characterize the governance of many agencies is a particular challenge and means that there is often no single point of accountability at the top level. Hence, efforts to design and implement organization-strengthening initiatives at an international level can be slow and problematic.

6. And finally, a significant challenge for INGOs is that **leadership, planning, and management practices** in the development sector have not kept pace with "good practice" with high-performing international organizations in the private sector. A particular aspect of this is the legacy of weak planning and performance management processes and disciplines, particularly at international levels. Too often, an approach based on simple line of sight management, with strong emphasis on established personal relationships, is at the heart of the organizational management approach.

Some INGOs, such as the World Wildlife Fund (WWF), have made considerable progress in this regard. However, established ideas like Kaplan and Norton's balanced scorecard concept,[10] which has long been adopted in various guises by successful international organizations, are only now beginning to be explored with any seriousness by INGOs. The real metrics for judging whether a unit of the organization is doing well are often too simplistic. Examples include the following:

- Have you spent all of your allocated funding in the allowed time frame?
- Have you provided the necessary reports and information demanded by donors?
- Have you minimized the percentage of expenditure that is not direct program investment?
- Have you managed to stay out of any audit "problem" lists?

We believe that much more robust frameworks need to be embraced with well-thought-through, consistent, and forward-looking metrics that encompass impact, quality programming, income and expenditure, people, knowledge and learning, and other key dimensions. This topic is a strong theme throughout this book and is explored more fully in chapter 6.

Emerging Pressures and Trends

In addition to these factors, there are a number of new and emerging pressures and trends also need to be considered by INGOs in relation to their structures. A few issues are becoming increasingly prominent.

1. There is an **increasing level of external scrutiny** of INGOs by external commentators, some informed and some not, in terms of the cost and effectiveness of programs. This is fueled by the growing focus of the global media on aid effectiveness and development issues in general. It is also fueled by the spread of technology, making it harder for INGOs to safeguard their reputation in the web and blog spheres.

2. The **role and contribution of international agencies are changing**, with a gradual move away from the "resource-transfer model" where agencies predominantly transfer resources from the more affluent North and use these to help deliver weak or missing services in the poorer South. Today, agencies are supporters and advocates of positive social and economic progress in poor countries at local, national, and international levels. The latter is arguably a less capital-intensive and more political and knowledge-intensive activity.

3. At a country program level, agencies are under more **pressure to increase their local legitimacy and independence**, which is likely to include the establishment of local governance structures, including independent local boards. However, INGOs are reluctant to move quickly in this direction because of the historic mind-set that cash is the scarce resource and hence "he who provides the cash, calls the shots." However, there is also a genuine concern that good local governance within developing countries may well be both slow and difficult to achieve in practice.

4. There are some **considerable shifts in the international political and economic environment**. An important aspect of this is the emergence of new centers of power and influence, not only India, China, and Brazil but also a raft of rapidly developing countries such as Indonesia, Mexico, South Africa, and South Korea. All of this is making the North and South distinction somewhat tired and outdated.

5. And, finally, with the **rapid advance in technological and particularly information technology capabilities**, the role of INGOs as intermediaries between well-off and poor countries is being challenged. This subject is explored in depth in chapter 4, "Reinventing International NGOs Through New Technology Possibilities."

3.3. Structural Variants: Pros and Cons

Having surveyed the context and range of particular characteristics, we will now review the range of structural options and variations that may be of interest for large INGOs. In examining these options, we also draw on ideas and models from large international organizations in the private sector. Later in the chapter we also explore the connection between structural variants and the impact of other important dimensions, such as processes, systems, skills, and leadership competence.

Structural Variants

Tables 3.2 and 3.3 illustrate seven models that could be considered. This is not a complete list, but it does represent a good cross-section of structures for INGOs to consider. In fact, some of these are variants of a matrix form, with differences in emphasis in terms of how power is assigned and exercised.

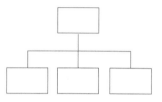

The first model, Model A, is the **traditional geographical or simple structure** referred to earlier. It has the significant advantage of being easy to understand, as the main lines of control and responsibility are, or at least seem to be, very clear. It often gives primacy to geography as the main line of control and power. In some cases, it might well recognize horizontal or cross-geography dimensions or areas of collaboration, though these are often fairly informal and not heavily represented in the real planning and decision-making processes.

Model B is the **line of business structure**. It is also a form of simple structure, but the main control lines are around lines of business, which are most likely to be designed around program categories. One could envisage a globally managed HIV and AIDS line of business or one for global microfinance programs. Employing this structure would offer an INGO the clear advantage of being able to adapt its skills, IT systems, and processes to the needs of that line of business and also to achieve greater quality through specialization. An agency using this model would also be better equipped to assist in vertical programs spanning multiple countries. However, a criticism would be that it is not sufficiently responsive to local contexts, where an integrated combination of interventions might be deemed most effective to achieve lasting improvements.

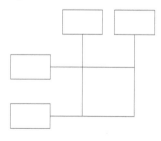

Model C, a **matrix structure**, is in reality a structural family with a number of variants. In one construct, it could comprise some combination of Model A and Model B. In this scenario there are explicit though overlapping lines of planning and management around geographical units and lines of business. Some staff would have dual reporting lines, which can arguably make decision making more complex. In practice, one of the dimensions assumes the stronger control for certain aspects of responsibility. The top leadership team or teams need to include representation from each of the dimensions of the matrix structure and take responsibility for dealing with trade-offs or conflicts.

The matrix form, which became prominent and controversial in the 1970s and 1980s, is now the norm for most large international corporations in the private sector. Frequently, these organizations evolve to exploit alternative forms of the matrix structure to meet specific priorities at different times. Often this means changing the power balance between different dimensions of the matrix to ensure a particular emphasis. An example of this is shifting the primary profit and loss responsibility from, say, a "geography" to a "line of business." In more sophisticated constructs, the matrix model can be designed to encompass dimensions including the following:

- geography: district, country, or region
- lines of business: product or service, program, or customer type
- skill or expertise area: technical or functional
- assets: physical or intellectual assets (e.g., in asset-intensive industries such as mining or oil and gas)

Model D, the **supply/demand model**, is another form of the matrix structure. It is particularly prevalent in sectors where people skills and expertise are the most critical assets and where there is value in a flexible and responsive mechanism that will match the key skills and expertise of the organization with the needs of particular projects or programs over time at national and international levels. In this model, a significant portion of program staff are employed by skill or competency units (supply) and rented to projects and programs for finite periods. The remainder of the staff sit in geographical or program units (demand), and as their needs at any given time dictate, they rent resources from the competency units for the duration of a particular program. The responsibility for recruitment, professional development, and long-term skills is the prime responsibility of the competency unit (supply). The short-term performance of an individual is a responsibility shared by the program units and the competency unit.

This type of approach is very common in professional service firms where skilled professional staff members are the key assets of the business, and their effective utilization, development, and performance are central to the success of the organization. In fact, we believe there are many parallels between these

(*text continues on p. 80*)

Table 3.2

Organizational Structure Variants and Summary Characteristics

Structural Variants		Characteristics
A. Traditional geographical or simple structure	Geographical units (e.g., headquarters [HQ], regions, and country programs) are the primary organizing structures of agency operations	• Fairly simple reporting structure • Majority of technical expertise and support functions embedded within geographic units • HQ technical and support functions work through consultation with other country and regional staff • Country or regional leads are the most prized and influential positions in the organization
B. Line of business structure	Organized globally according to program types or domains of activity (e.g., emergency response, health, education, microfinance)	• Most key resources owned by lines of business • Emphasis on quality through focus and specialization • Adapt management process, support functions, and style of organization to needs of each line of business so potentially less consistency or standardization across different lines of business
C. Some form of matrix structure	All key dimensions of geography, program domains, skill domains, and support functions are formally recognized in executive leadership structure	• Organizational units have dual or multiple reporting lines according to geography, line of business, skill domain, or functional area, although typically one dimension will take a stronger lead than the others on particular aspects • Flat leadership team structure representing all important dimensions • Frequently executives take more than one responsibility for different nodes of management • Requires integrated approach to planning, objective setting, and performance management • Requires strong, well-defined HR performance management processes to facilitate multiple reporting lines

D. Supply/demand model	Slimmed down line structure (Model A or B) with the majority of program and technical staff in competency units (supply) and assigned as required on a project basis to program leads (demand)	• Key program or technical staff loaned or rented to countries, regions, or lines of business on a project-by-project basis • Subset of management and staff retained in country or lines of business and, as required, called off capacity and expertise from competency units • Individual performance management is a shared activity between line managers and competency managers
E. Shared services model	Provision of support services on a shared regional or global basis, from the lowest cost or most effective location	• Formal service management agreements between service provider and customers of services, setting out scope, nature, and levels of services provided, as well as prearranged charging arrangements
F. Strategic mini-regions (or regional hubs)	Grouping together small clusters of countries (e.g., two to five countries) of similar geography, context, or need into mini-regions or regional hubs	• Shared technical expertise and support functions for small clusters of countries with similar contexts and needs • Economies of scale in selected management positions • Simplifying the overall management of the agency to a smaller number of manageable country clusters
G. Country federation	Increased autonomy and local governance of each country program to be able to adapt more fully to local needs	• Extreme version of Model A but significantly more autonomy in terms of local strategy and execution at country level, with strong local governance • Very limited central control and coordination

Table 3.3

Organizational Structure Variants: Pros and Cons

Structural Variants	Good For	Not So Good For
A. Traditional geographical or simple structure	• Clarity and speed of decision making • Flexibility to adapting to local context • Small organizations, particularly with narrow focus of activity	• Managing larger, interdependent international programs and activities • Sharing of best practice • Standardization of processes and practices • Best use of scarce resources and expertise
B. Line of business structure	• Where lines of business have low interdependence • Where a strong central, global entity can manage and maintain the motivating glue of the organization (mission, values, culture) • Where lines of business are very large scale and can justify own support and management systems	• Integrated program design and implementation in the field • Flexibility to adapt the preferred focus of programs to reflect local needs • Consistency and sharing of support functions and technical expertise • Avoiding duplication in support functions
C. Some form of matrix structure	• Integrated planning and decision making • Mobility of resources and expertise to areas of highest priority and/or need • Where leadership style is naturally collaborative and oriented to longer-term planning horizons	• Where speed of reaction is more important than integration and consistency • Where integrated planning and key support processes and systems are weak
D. Supply/demand model	• Matching key resources with areas of greatest need on an international basis • Avoiding stranding key expertise in a node of the organization	• Where longer-term deployment of key expertise to local geographical context is an important contributor to program success

	• Combining short-term project performance and longer-term competency strengthening into performance management and career development activities	• Agencies without strong processes for balancing supply and demand and allocating resources • Agencies without the ability to track people, time, and costs and link these to project management processes
E. Shared services model	• Delivery of services across multiple organization units to achieve the benefits of economies of scale that result from a larger service delivery model • Customer requirements are stable and can be clearly defined • Can establish productive supplier/customer relationship with positive incentives and behaviors	• Nature of services required across different customer groups are very different with potentially fragmented needs • Unstable requirements, not easy to define • Scale of services needed is low • Management behavior not conducive to creating a positive service provider/customer relationship
F. Strategic mini-regions (or regional hubs)	• There are economies of scale for technical expertise/support functions across countries • Linking with local regional issues and stakeholders • Ability to contribute to need in countries/areas of need where there is no full country office • Giving national staff a route to a broader contribution outside their country of origin	• Country presence, independence, and self-sufficiency is paramount in program effectiveness
G. Country federation	• Countries where local NGOs are preferred by donors and local stakeholders (dislike taking direction from international NGOs) • Where there is a strong "influencing policy and practice" dimension to programs	• Standardization and sharing of best practice • Economies of scale and consistency of supporting/enabling processes • Implementing international programs

firms and international development agencies, and hence this form merits serious consideration for the longer term.

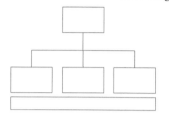
Model E, the **shared services model**, is another variant of the matrix form and also can overlap with some of the other models. This model responds to pressures for greater cost-effectiveness, standardization, and professionalism of key support processes such as finance and accounting, human resources, and information technology. The theory is that shared provision of these services on a regional or global basis will provide better economies of scale and support the necessary investment in the standardization and strengthening of these processes.

It should also allow for the provision of these services from the location with the lowest cost and/or best capability to provide the service. This is indeed a model with some merit, although it needs to be considered carefully in relation to some of the basic requirements for a successful shared services or outsourcing model. These requirements include (1) sufficient scale to justify the cost of establishing and managing a shared services operation, (2) stability of requirements or customer needs to be able to establish a reasonably stable and manageable service provision contract, and (3) maturity of management to be, in effect, mature buyers of the shared services being offered. Outsourcing is the extreme form of this option and does have some merit for certain support processes.

Model F, **strategic mini-regions**, is a specific variant that could include aspects of many of the other models. In this scenario, the INGO could create a new localized strategic clustering of countries (say two to five) based on similarity of context, culture, political landscape, need, language, or geography. This mini-region or "regional hub" could be managed on an integrated basis, with support functions and technical and project expertise shared across individual program countries. This creates the opportunity to exploit genuine local economies of scale and also deliver pan-country programs more effectively across the mini-region.

Creation of mini-regions could also generate a more manageable number of geographical units to coordinate internationally. In addition, local economies of scale should allow central functions at global headquarters to limit their remit to areas such as brand, organizational growth, core program methodology, and overall allocation of scarce resources. This approach could, therefore, offer the opportunity to keep the international coordination and alignment costs (overhead) to a minimum.

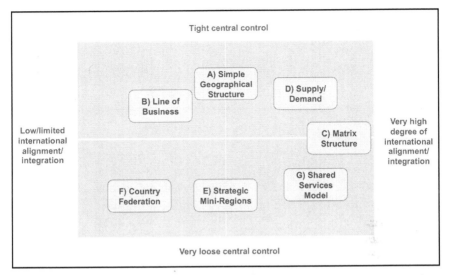

Figure 3.1 Organizational variants mapped against degree of central control and international alignment.

Model G, the **country federation**, is a model that responds to the view that international economies of scale and the value of deeper international integration are less important than local flexibility and autonomy. In this model there is limited appetite for standardization, alignment, and common approaches.

These various alternatives are not mutually exclusive. Figure 3.1 shows the models mapped onto a simple grid according to the degree of central control that might be related to the variant (vertical axis), as well as the degree of international alignment/integration sought (horizontal axis). By plotting the different variants, it is possible to see that each can potentially be located in a variety of positions on the grid. The simple geographical structure is most likely to be on the center or toward the left side of the grid, though its vertical positioning may vary depending on the organization and also on individual perspective. For example, country program teams may feel there is a high degree of central control, while central management may feel that country programs have considerable, perhaps too much, autonomy.

The degree of integration of a country federation model depends on the nature of the federation agreement but is most likely to be at the lower left side of the grid. An effective matrix structure should be strong on integration but could present itself as having a low degree of central control, depending on the strength and maturity of key planning and management processes. It also needs to have a group of leaders who demonstrate the required capacity, behaviors, and, importantly, trust to be able to lead and manage effectively in this environment.

3.4. Managing Structural Change for International NGOs

The right structural configuration for any organization will almost certainly depend on the context, history, people, and, particularly, the most important strategic priorities of that organization at that time. The journey toward a satisfactory model is therefore likely to be an iterative one, with a number of different factors needing to be synchronized along the journey.

Factors Needing to Be Synchronized

Figure 3.2 sets out some of the factors that are particularly relevant to consider when designing the journey to becoming a more effective INGO. As this diagram seeks to illustrate, one of the real challenges is to develop the leadership behaviors, as well as the planning and management disciplines, that are required in order to become a very effective, high-performing INGO, almost irrespective to the choice of structural model. These dimensions are too often not sufficiently advanced to meet the needs of agencies today.

Figure 3.2 Synchronization of structural changes with other key dimensions.

Another very important factor is the expectations of external partners who want agencies to be aligned and responsive, on both a local basis and an international basis. This expectation also places additional pressures on the scale and sophistication of international programs, which in turn places demands on the structure and the enabling processes.

Understanding the Glue

Structure is about aligning each part of the organization to contribute effectively to the delivery of the overall mission. It includes the order and discipline necessary to achieve this aim. However, structure is also an important contributor to the glue that binds everyone in the organization together to focus on the delivery of that mission.

In the planning and management of change, we believe it is important to gain a deep understanding of this glue and ensure that it is strengthened in the process of change, not undermined. For the purposes of simplification, we believe there are two broad categories of glue: enabling glue and motivating glue.

The **enabling glue** is well understood and is often the subject of organizational strengthening programs, which can sometimes be seen as difficult, expensive, and time consuming to undertake. In addition, many staff, despite understanding the importance of these areas, are not always greatly inspired by initiatives aimed at establishing stronger financial management, more rigorous human resources management processes, or better monitoring and evaluation systems. However, we all know that these are critical aspects and need to be strong and effective for a large INGO to operate effectively.

On the other hand, there is often a risk that insufficient attention is given to the **motivating glue** that is also vital to understand, strengthen, and nourish. This is a critical aspect for any organization, especially for development and relief agencies (sometimes referred to as the "secret sauce"). In fact it is a central part of why staff choose this work for their career, often with modest remuneration and at considerable sacrifice to their family lives. This is what gives staff a real connection with, and loyalty to, their organization.

Hence, a well-designed change process needs to have a reasonable balance of effort aimed at strengthening the enabling glue of the organization and at the same time nurturing the motivating glue that is so essential to the morale and performance of the workforce. Where programs are designed to strengthen the main enabling components, it is important that the benefits of these are connected as much as possible to the components of the motivating glue. This will increase the chances that staff will embrace the changes proposed.

Motivating Glue

- Mission and identity
- Organization's specific contribution to the development process
- Camaraderie with like-minded, high-caliber, loyal staff with similar values
- Quality programs and impact in the field

Enabling Glue

- Program design standards, guidelines, and methodology
- Program monitoring and evaluation (processes, systems, and expertise)
- Financial processes and systems
- HR processes and systems
- Talent management
- Knowledge management tools, processes, and systems
- Business planning and performance management

Rebalancing the Time of Senior Executives

In the evolution to a more sophisticated, modern INGO, how will the time of senior executives be spent differently? This is an important question. Being a leader in a more effective, sophisticated international organization, most likely with some form of matrix structure, will require a very different style of management and leadership, as shown in the following changes:

- Executives will be working with a much broader and most likely flatter top team structure, with many more dimensions of the matrix represented in the top management teams.
- By implication, executives will not be able to keep abreast of all of the detailed issues, along every dimension. Instead, they will need to trust the responsible leads to deliver their area's contribution to the organization's performance and rely on the systematic planning and performance processes to spot issues and interventions.
- It is likely that many of the leaders of the new broader team will be dispersed across multiple locations in multiple countries, North and South, implying much less face-to-face contact and relying on virtual forms of communication.
- The mode of management and accountability will shift from the informal, line of sight, and sometimes command and control approach to a much more coaching style supported by well-

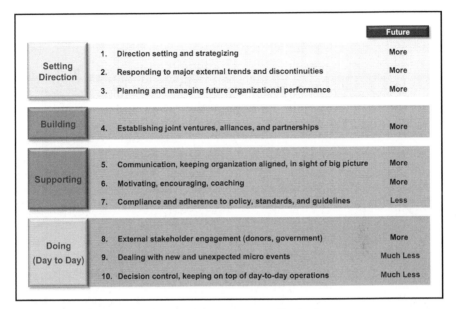

Figure 3.3 Changing emphasis: Executive management and leadership.

structured and transparent planning and performance management processes.

- All managers and staff throughout the agency will need to get comfortable with the idea or mind-set of dual citizenship, that is, being equally committed to the performance of the total organization while retaining ownership for the performance of their own specific area of responsibility or their own part of the organization.

Figure 3.3 gives a high-level representation of the likely shift in the way that senior executive management allocates its time. In summary, we envisage much less emphasis on day-to-day operational issues and considerably more on setting strategic direction, managing the performance of the agency, and building or strengthening the agency for the future.

3.5. Conclusions

Observations of INGOs and the lessons drawn from decades of thought about organizational structures and performance lead us to conclude that there is no single correct answer. The right structural configuration for any organization is almost certain to depend on its context, history, people, and strategic priorities.

However, what is also clear is that the simple geographical structure, which is still a common format for many INGOs, is no longer equipped to deal with the scope and scale of their activities, which today include an increasingly complex array of programs, geographies, donors, and partners. The best model seems to be one that will allow local flexibility and autonomy to pursue opportunities and take decisions at local levels while at the same time being more effective in facilitating the consistent approaches and shared learning that can be gained from being part of a large international organization.

In summary, we would like to draw out the following six high-level observations.

1. The traditional, simple geographical structure, with a command and control style of management, is not well equipped to deal with the reality of an INGO in today's context. **Some form of matrix model is inevitable**, though the degree of complexity and sophistication that can be achieved may need to evolve over an extended period of five to ten years.

2. As INGOs progress toward the target structure they deem most desirable, it is important they **recognize the essential dimensions that need to be considered and progressed in a synchronized manner**. This will give them the best chance of achieving the high-performing global structure they desire. These prerequisite dimensions are likely to include management and leadership skills and behaviors, planning and management processes and disciplines, and also a number of key enabling processes and systems.

3. The process of becoming a high-performing international organization is iterative, and could be both an evolutionary process and a revolutionary process. However, evolution could benefit from a number of many mini-revolutions over an extended period.

4. As organizations pursue the process of change, it is critical that they balance efforts to **nurture and strengthen the motivating glue** for these organizations, in addition to continued efforts to strengthen the enabling glue. Care should be taken to avoid excessive emphasis on the **enabling glue**, which may not be a strong motivator for all staff, at the expensive of those factors that build commitment and esprit de corps (the motivating glue).

5. International development agencies are more akin to venture capitalists than automotive makers. Despite all the narrative to the contrary, it is all too easy to fall into the trap that suggests that international development is a predictable and repeatable process with expected outcomes and impacts that can be fully anticipated and tracked. They cannot. Put another way, the notion

of a top-down, heavily planned social and economic progress has rarely been a formula for success.

6. It is important to appreciate the **role that structure plays in supporting and nurturing the most critical core competencies** of an organization. Structural form plays a considerable role in promoting and hindering (unfortunately more typically) the most important core competencies that are the bedrock of any organization's future.

Notes

1. F. W. Taylor, *The Principles of Scientific Management* (New York: Harper, 1911).

2. Henry Ford and Samuel Crowther, *My Life and Work* (Garden City, NY: Garden City Publishing Company, 1922).

3. J. Galbraith, *Designing Complex Organizations and Organization Design* (Reading, MA: Addison-Wesley, 1977); H. Mintzberg, *The Structuring of Organizations* (Englewood Cliffs, NJ: Prentice Hall, 1979).

4. Mintzberg, *The Structuring of Organizations.*

5. Michael Porter, *Competitive Strategy: Techniques for Analyzing Industries and Competitors* (New York: Free Press, 1980).

6. C. K. Prahalad and Gary Hamel, "The Core Competence of the Corporation," *Harvard Business Review* (May–June 1990): 79–90.

7. Thomas J. Peters and Robert H. Waterman, *In Search of Excellence* (New York: Harper and Row, 1982).

8. Jim Collins, *Good to Great: Why Some Companies Make the Leap . . . and Others Don't* (New York: Collins Business, 2001) and *Good to Great and the Social Sectors: A Monograph to Accompany Good to Great* (London: Random House Business Books, 2006).

9. D. R. Kingdon, *Matrix Organization* (London: Tavistock, 1973).

10. Robert S. Kaplan and David P. Norton, "The Balanced Scorecard: Measures That Drive Performance," *Harvard Business Review* (January–February 1992): 71–79.

Reinventing International NGOs
Through New Technology
Possibilities

Abstract

Information and communication technologies (ICTs) present enormous opportunity for significant progress across the developing world. They can make a very real difference in the lives of the poor in both rural and urban contexts. New opportunities are being facilitated by the breathtaking pace of penetration of mobile telephony and Internet in the developing world. This is supporting many new possibilities, including innovative breakthroughs in important sectors such as agriculture, health, education, and microfinance. Rapid technology adoption is helping to advance local and international trade. It also provides new, innovative ways of communicating and lobbying that transcend international borders.

With this growing momentum, international NGOs (INGOs) are, in theory, well positioned to influence how effectively and quickly ICT is utilized for the benefit of the poor. Through their field programs and local partners, INGOs have a deep understanding and a close working relationship with the poor on the ground, with local communities, with local district and national government bodies, and, increasingly, with the business community. Through their international program teams, INGOs also have the potential to test, share, and develop ideas and new approaches, allowing them to build on successes and avoid repeated pitfalls.

However, the experience to date in terms of the use of ICT for development programs (ICT4D) supported by INGOs is not encouraging. Progress has been ad hoc, with many small initiatives or pilots but few sustainable, large-scale examples. Arguably, many INGOs are not well equipped to support and nurture the effective exploitation of ICT for the benefit of the poor.

This chapter is divided roughly into two parts, each offering a contrasting view of what ICT means for INGOs. In the first part, we explore the impact of ICT with a "glass half full" perspective and review these new ICT opportunities, be they incremental or radical, making an implicit assumption that INGOs can embrace these possibilities. We include illustrative examples, as much as possible, to bring to life the richness and the power of what it is increasingly possible to achieve.

The second part of this chapter takes a more critical "glass half empty" perspective, challenging whether the new possibilities driven by ICT could be considered as a disruptive technology and potentially lead to the demise of the large established INGOs we know today. In this section, we draw on the ideas and insights from the valuable research of Clayton M. Christensen and his book *The Innovator's Dilemma*. In this work, he makes a very interesting distinction between **sustaining** technologies, which help incumbents improve their products and operations, and **disruptive** technologies, which can, despite management's best efforts, lead to the failure of even the strongest and well-managed organizations.

4.1. Introduction

Information and communications technology (ICT) represents an enormous opportunity to introduce significant and lasting positive change across the developing world. The rapid penetration of mobile access in particular has resulted in considerable improvements in the lives of the poor in both rural and urban contexts. All evidence suggests that this trend is going to continue, as the availability expands and the cost of access continues to decline.[1]

A Wave of Tremendous Opportunity

The changes and new possibilities that ICT offers span most areas of international development and are facilitated by the breathtaking pace of penetration and uptake of mobile telephony and broadband Internet. This is supporting many new possibilities, products, and services; providing breakthrough ideas in agriculture, health, education, and access to finance; and helping local and international trade. It also provides new breakthrough ways of communicating and lobbying, which transcends international borders, as shown by the role of mobile phones and the Internet in the waves of revolution that spread across Northern Africa in 2011.

An Internet search using the phrase "information and communications technology for development" (ICT4D) produces an overwhelming volume of literature, with many exciting examples that promise enormous possibilities. ICT is changing the landscape whether we like it or not, and despite its somewhat erratic progress to date, the influence is increasingly profound.

With this growing momentum, INGOs are, in theory, well positioned to influence how effectively and quickly ICT is utilized to benefit the poor and the disadvantaged. Through their field programs and local partners, INGOs have a deep understanding and a close working relationship with the poor on the ground, with district and national government bodies, and, increasingly, with the business community at local, national, and international levels. In addition, through their international program teams, they have the potential to test, share, and develop valuable knowledge networks that can assist them to spread valuable learning, build on successes, and avoid pitfalls.

Five Key Challenges

However, this new potential and opportunity is accompanied by significant challenges and possible threats for large established INGOs.

First, the use of ICT in development programs supported by INGOs has, to date, been relatively ad hoc, with many examples of small initiatives

or pilots but very few large-scale, sustainable, ICT-supported programs. To unleash the full potential of ICT in development programs, a new level of collaboration, both internally and with other organizations, and a new approach to scaling solutions to achieve a really material impact are needed. This will necessitate significant coordination between INGOs, technology companies, private sector organizations, universities, and government entities (central and local), as well as with traditional development partners.

Second, many INGOs are not well equipped internally to support and nurture the effective exploitation of ICT to benefit development. They simply do not have the knowledge, expertise, or organizational capacity needed. The use of information technology is often seen as a thorny, problematic issue relating to back office systems. Furthermore, ICT often has a questionable reputation as a result of previous unsuccessful or costly initiatives.

Third, INGOs' current structures, staffing, and ways of operating have a strong momentum that is not easy to halt or redirect. It is relatively easy to utilize ICT to sustain and improve current organizational constructs and approaches, making useful but incremental progress. It is incredibly difficult to conceive of new ways of working with organizational constructs that are fundamentally different from the status quo and require a shift in terms of strategy, competence, skills, and organizational structure.

There also is a significant challenge in adequately planning and financing the use of ICT in development programs. With cyclical donor funding and pressure to minimize administrative and management costs, it is often difficult for INGOs to properly plan and resource financial and human investments in ICT as a core capacity for development programs.

Finally, the emergence of new ICT possibilities potentially presents some more fundamental and far-reaching questions, challenging or even undermining the assumptions on which INGOs came into being. When we reflect on why INGOs were originally founded, we can isolate a number of specific gaps between people and communities in poverty and those in more affluent, developed parts of the world. For example, if we think about gaps around understanding and information, traditionally INGOs helped us understand the dire need of communities in the poorest parts of the world. There are also gaps in terms of access, communication, and of course resources that INGOs have historically played an important role in addressing.

While some of these gaps still exist, they are, arguably, not as clear or compelling as they once were. We can see that developments and possibilities created through ICT, directly and indirectly, materially change the landscape in relation to many of these gaps.

Looking at these five challenges, we can paint two broad and very different perspectives, building on the useful distinction set out by Clayton M. Christensen in the very insightful book *The Innovator's Dilemma*,[2] first published in 1997. In this book, the author makes a very important distinction between sustaining technologies, which help incumbents to improve, and disruptive technologies, which can ultimately lead to the failure of strong incumbents despite their very best efforts to continuously enhance their products, improve their cost competiveness, and listen carefully to the needs of their most important customers. The paradox of large, established, and successful organizations is that they have virtually all of the assets—money, brands, intellectual property, facilities, momentum—yet their natural dominance is frequently overturned by upstarts.

How is it that emerging organizations with minimal resources can defeat huge established players? In his research Christensen explores whether it is possible for executives to simultaneously do what is right for the near-term health of their established organizations and focus adequate resources to address the disruptive technologies that could otherwise lead to the organization's downfall.

Following similar lines of thinking as Christensen, we broadly divided the rest of this chapter into two parts, each offering a contrasting view of the role and impact of ICT possibilities in the developing world, and specifically on what ICT means for INGOs.

In the first part (sections 4.2 and 4.3), we explore the more optimistic "glass half full" perspective, which loosely treats these new ICT possibilities, be they incremental or radical, as sustaining technologies. It makes an implicit assumption that INGOs can embrace these possibilities and continue to have an important role to play and contribution to make. We survey the broad range of ICT ideas and possibilities. We included illustrative examples, as much as possible, to bring to life the richness and the power of what it is increasingly possible to achieve. As we review this exciting range of trends and possibilities, we also explore what INGOs need to do to maximize the opportunities presented.

In the subsequent part (section 4.4), we take a more critical look at these new ICT possibilities. We ask if they could endanger the longevity of established INGOs and hence if they may effectively be termed disruptive technologies, facilitating the emergence of new and different kinds of organizations and contributing to the demise of some of the large established INGOs we know today.

In section 4.5, we bring the two strands together and draw some broad conclusions and recommendations targeted particularly at how established

INGOs can best embrace this set of new ICT possibilities, be they sustaining or disruptive in nature.

4.2. Trends and Possibilities for ICT for Development (ICT4D)

In February 2010, the United Nations International Telecommunication Union (UN ITU) report "Measuring the Information Society Report 2010"[3] reviewed the price of mobile and Internet access in 159 countries to create the ICT Development Index. The results of the study showed interesting trends, most notably that "despite the recent economic downturn, the use of ICT services has continued to grow worldwide"[4] in both the developed and the developing worlds. Figures collected as part of the ICT Development Index show the strong upward trend in access to both mobile cellular and Internet, as illustrated in figure 4.1.

Penetration of Mobile and Internet in the Developing World

A few notable trends in relation to mobile cellular technology in the developing world were highlighted in the UN ITU report:

- Mobile technology is the main driver of ICT growth.

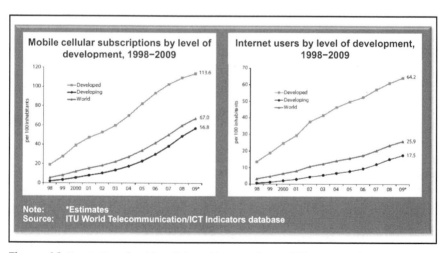

Figure 4.1 Penetration of mobile cellular and Internet. *Source.* UN International Telecommunication Union, "Measuring the Information Society Report 2010," February 23, 2010.

- Mobile penetration has more than doubled since 2005, and it's estimated that 57 percent of inhabitants in the developing world have subscriptions.
- Mobile telephony subscriptions appear to be fairly resilient to economic fluctuations.
- Between 2008 and 2009, the cost of ICT access and usage as a percentage of gross national income per capita has dropped by an average of 15 percent.

Also highlighted in the report were some notable Internet trends in the developing world:

- Internet continues to expand impressively, though at a slower pace than mobile.
- There was 18 percent Internet penetration in the developing world by 2009, although this drops to 14 percent if China is excluded. China has more than half of the fixed broadband subscribers in the developing world.
- In 2008, China overtook the United States as the largest fixed broadband market in the world.

The following observation from the UN ITU paper is a good indication of the extent to which ICT does have the potential to help close the gap between the developing world and the developed world and support a real step change:[5]

> In 2008, mobile cellular penetration and fixed broadband penetration in developing countries had reached the level that Sweden (ranking first in the ICT Development Index) had almost a decade earlier, and the number of Internet users per 100 inhabitants was the same as Sweden's just over 11 years earlier. In contrast, life expectancy in developing countries is lagging Sweden by 66 years, and the infant mortality in developing countries in 2007 was at the same level where Sweden stood 72 years earlier.

Uses of ICT in Development (ICT4D)

The practical use of ICT in development programs varies considerably across sectors such as health, education, and agriculture. Usually, the improvement will be in one or both of the following areas: (1) work that is aimed at **improving impact for beneficiaries** (e.g., sending medical reminders, providing access to market information) and (2) work that is aimed at **improving the efficiency of the program activities** (e.g., automating the data collection process can save time and result in better-quality information to support better decision making).

However, for the purposes of this chapter, the following six broad types of ICT uses have been defined to categorize the kinds of uses of ICT to support development and relief activities across all sectors:[6]

- **Remote data collection:** Use of technology to manage a one-way collection of data. A good example of this is the collection of survey information from farmers or community workers in remote communities.
- **Education and awareness:** Use of technology to facilitate a two-way exchange of information. Examples include providing answers to questions about market prices and sending medical reminders or messages to indicate the arrival of emergency supplies.
- **Communications and training:** Use of technology to support multiway communications. For example, ICT can be helpful when training groups of farmers, as you need to have up-to-date training material, be able to share it with learners, and be able to update it.
- **Analysis and reporting:** Use of technology to support data analysis and reporting. Examples include reviewing data on crop health and generating reports in a format that others can access.
- **Tracking:** Use of technology (including geographic information or mapping systems) to monitor and track information and trends in multiple areas, including supply chain and geographic mapping. Examples include using technology to track and monitor the distribution of emergency response food and equipment and also to track the spread of a plant disease outbreak.
- **Remote services:** Use of technology to provide community services such as banking services, patient diagnostics, or postdisaster reunification services.

Having considered, at an overall level, the various uses of ICT in development, it is useful to look more specifically at how ICT can be used to support and transform programs in the various sectors. As illustrated in figure 4.2, these uses touch all the sectors in which most INGOs work. Some of the

Program Sectors / Tech. Purposes	AGRICULTURE	HEALTH	EMERGENCY	MICROFINANCE	EDUCATION	WATER & SANITATION	PEACE BUILDING
Remote Data Collection	Seed distribution, crop levels	Patient information	Impact resulting from emergency	Gather info on buying and business habits	Student and teacher information	Water quality, tree planting	Criminal intelligence data
Education and Awareness (provide information)	Access to market prices, weather, literacy	Medical reminders	Arrival of emergency supplies	Availability and usage of online mobile banking	Availability and usage of online educational materials	WASH education messages	Awareness of local events/ issues
Communication and Training (multiway dialogue)	Field agents capacity	Health worker capacity	Alert and co-ord. systems, online bulletin boards	Customized ATMs	Teacher training, online educational communities	WASH training	Election participation/ results
Analysis and Reporting	Crop levels, hunger and malnutrition analysis	Patient adherence analysis	Threat and risk-mapping analysis	Mobile portfolio management	Education information and management	Sustainable energy, carbon offset	Security monitoring
Tracking (e.g., geographic information)	Plant varieties, plant diseases, food distribution	Epidemics, medical supply distribution	Disaster assessments, supply chain	Tracking customer base	School locations, distribution of school supplies	Geospatial mapping	Peace Incidents
Remote Services	Plant diseases	Patient diagnostics	Reunification, finding job opportunities	Money transfer, banking services	Diet lectoring certificates	Infrastructure and diagnosis	Early warning

Figure 4.2 Example uses of ICT4D by sector.

solutions are specific to a sector, but others can run across multiple sectors. This is an indicative illustration and does not necessarily contain every possible combination of ICT purpose and program sector usage, especially when you consider how quickly new pilots and examples are being created every day. We will now consider each sector in a little more detail.

Use of ICT by Sector

Agriculture, along with health, was one of the first areas where the benefits of the mobile revolution were identified as a means to support greater program impact. Access to market pricing via mobile phones for farmers and fishermen has proved to be a useful means to obtain accurate pricing information to ensure that local producers get a fair deal. This has expanded into farmer "help lines" that focus on information about crop production techniques, crop health, and animal health.

A very good example is the Great Lakes Cassava Initiative, which is an innovative and dynamic partnership between Catholic Relief Services, academic institutions, technology companies, and the Bill & Melinda Gates Foundation.[7] This program is accelerating the process of distributing healthy cassava plants and educating farmer groups on cassava crop disease. It is also researching cassava crop disease across six countries in Africa in a quest to build a sustainable solution to the problem that is currently threatening the food security of many communities. This case study is illustrated further in figure 4.3.

In the **health sector**, there are numerous examples of the application of ICT4D to help health professionals and also directly help patients. For health professionals, opportunities exist in the area of detailed data capture and analysis, which usually requires computer-based, fairly sophisticated ICT solutions. For patients, ICT health solutions usually make use of mobile phones and thus are referred to as mHealth (mobile health). Examples include simple one-way communications, such as reminding HIV/AIDS patients to take their medication, through to more advanced solutions, such as the use of mobile phones with video functionality to record and send footage of patients taking medication.[8]

Over the past couple of years, the number of examples of ICT being applied in health programs has increased significantly. In 2008, there were over a dozen new mHealth applications being implemented or trialed.[9] The formation of the mHealth Alliance in 2009 through the joint efforts of the UN Foundation and Vodafone Foundation signaled serious intent to approach ICT in health in a more integrated way. This is quite important given the evidence that scale and sustainability are key elements in successfully transitioning from pilot to long-term, life-changing solutions. NetHope, a unique collaboration of the world's leading international humanitarian organizations working together to utilize IT to solve common problems in the developing world, has also been working in this area to develop a global health platform.[10] This platform provides a standard way to gather data and share information. Achieving scale and sustainability is something that will be covered more in a later section of this chapter, but it is particularly relevant in the health sector.

In **education**, there is considerable excitement about the possibilities of electronic learning (eLearning) for multiple purposes: to improve general literacy, improve skills and knowledge in various sectors, to harmonize testing methods and improve standards, and also to overcome teacher shortages. Increasingly common is the ability to download entire books to local devices, as well as to use mobile technology to deliver digital multimedia materials to teachers and students. And, of course, the increasing ability to exploit solar power is a considerable help in many remote, off-grid areas.

In the area of **microfinance**, the number of people with a phone but without a bank account is large and expected to reach 1.7 billion by 2012.[11] There are some great examples of mobile banking (mBanking) with m-PESA in Kenya and GCash in the Philippines, though admittedly, they are not without challenges, particularly in terms of regulation.

Catholic Relief Services (CRS), funded by the Bill & Melinda Gates Foundation, is managing a four-year program focused on cassava crop health across the six countries surrounding the Great Lakes. The program is a complex mix of cassava crop research, distribution of healthy crop cuttings, farmer group education, and monitoring and evaluation (M&E) analysis. CRS, utilizing its association with NetHope, has formed a relationship with Intel around the supply of ruggedized laptops for the program.

These ruggedized laptops, designed to work in harsh environments, include cassava crop health training courses using Agilix BrainHoney, a learning management application, and M&E forms. They run in online and offline mode to cope with intermittent connectivity across the six countries. The laptops are in the hands of approximately 250 CRS partner-staff across the six countries. Partner-staff complete a one-week face-to-face training course to learn how to use the ruggedized laptop and how to navigate the BrainHoney training. They then complete the training courses on the laptops and use the courses to educate farmer groups in five key skill areas. While they are visiting farmer groups, M&E information is captured and photos of the cassava crops are gathered. All this information can be viewed centrally by the program management team and used to support decision making about the program and the spread of cassava crop disease.

This is an example of a complex functional requirement, a very sector-specific solution, and the development of innovative new partnerships and relationships at a global level with Intel and NetHope, and local-level contracts with IT companies in the six countries who provide support and maintenance for the laptops and applications.

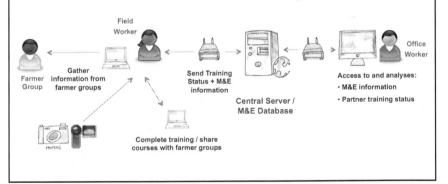

Figure 4.3 Case example: Great Lakes Cassava Initiative.

In the area of **emergency response**, we see a range of applications of ICT. The use of one-way remote data collection via crowd sourcing solutions like Ushahidi has been shown to have increasing effect as evidenced in the 2010–2011 North Africa and Middle East uprisings. There are also very advanced applications of ICT around the tracking and management of supply chains associated with the distribution of emergency supplies during a crisis situation.

An interesting instance of this is an example we came across in the early aftermath of a disaster, where a major telecommunications company in Indonesia made a pledge to have a local network of telecommunications masts in place within eight hours of a tsunami or earthquake situation. This provides the critical mobile communication to enable relief workers to coordinate and manage the relief efforts in the critical early stages. Another example is the use of navigation and mapping tools (GPS and Google Earth) for both prevention and response activities.

This is just a small snapshot of the many different functional and sectoral uses of ICT. What is clear is the pervasive and even daunting nature of the role of ICT in contributing to the development process. While it is an exciting opportunity, it is also a challenge when one considers the significant issues involved in the planning and implementation of large-scale solutions, which we will touch on in the next section. Selecting a suitable solution, a set of complementary partners, and an implementation approach for your program is not without its challenges. But considering the possibility to transform the pace and magnitude of impact compared to what was possible even one decade ago, the challenge seems to be a very worthwhile one.

4.3. Making Opportunities Count: The Three Ss—Support, Scale, and Sustainability

With growing momentum in the use of ICT in development programs comes an awareness of the challenges related to making ICT4D programs successful, taking ICT4D solutions to scale, and ensuring their long-term support and sustainability. While there is a significant amount of literature sharing examples of pilot and single programs using ICT4D, there is a resounding silence in the area of ICT4D support, scale, and sustainability.

Yet without addressing these aspects, INGOs and other development sector players are missing the potential that ICT has for delivering a step change. In this section we discuss key areas INGOs need to consider when designing programs with a significant ICT component.

Components of ICT4D Solutions

An ICT4D solution is not a single component but a number of component parts. Careful mixing and matching of these based on the function and sectoral focus of the program is important in the design of workable solutions. And of course, the availability of communications networks is also very important. First, we will summarize the main components of an ICT4D solution. These are set out in figure 4.4. We then review the types of organizations that need to come together to deliver large-scale solutions. And finally, we will look at some key lessons in planning programs that use ICT in a significant way.

At a summary level, a typical ICT4D solution comprises the following component parts:

- **Devices—hardware:** the front-end devices that are used to run the ICT solution. This includes devices such as mobile phones, tablets, laptops, Global Positioning System (GPS) units, cameras, video recorders, and digital pens.
- **Devices—software:** the applications and forms developed to run on the device's hardware. For example, a survey application that runs on a mobile phone.
- **Communications networks:** the means by which information is transmitted from the front-end hardware and software devices

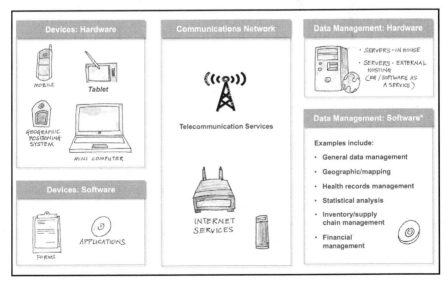

Figure 4.4 Overview of the main components of an ICT4D solution.

to the back-end data management devices. This can include mobile networks, Internet networks, and USB drives. The quality of mobile and Internet connectivity in a program location can significantly impact the design of the selected ICT solution. Designing ICT solutions that work in online and offline modes is one way to deal with connectivity challenges.

- **Data management—hardware:** the servers that capture information and store it. Historically, servers were owned and managed by the INGO, but as the world increasingly moves to "the cloud," there are options for software as a service where a third party hosts the server and provides access.
- **Data management—software:** the applications that sit on the server and support the analysis and reporting and storage of information that has been captured. Software solutions can range from general-purpose relational database packages to specific-use systems such as inventory management or health records management.

Range of Contributing Organizations and Partners

What types of organizations need to come together to support large-scale ICT4D initiatives? One of the bigger challenges to achieve maximum positive impact from the use of ICT4D is to bring together the best thinking and expertise from a range of partners, to bring these projects to scale, and then to support (and resource) the solutions on an ongoing basis as they evolve and scale up.

This collaboration needs to be developed in a way that puts the needs and benefits of poor communities at the heart of efforts so that this does not get lost in the frenzy of collaboration and partnership agreements that is inevitable between larger stakeholders. Clearly, large-scale solutions need to be anchored in local communities, as well as integrated with government (local and central) activities and initiatives.

They also need to be supported by, as much as possible, local private sector providers and other local institutions or universities. For example, in the health sector, the limited literature that does exist indicates that it is programs with ICT that are aligned to the community- or country-level government health strategy that are much more likely to get long-term, in-country support and be more sustainable than those that rely only on donor funding cycles.[12]

There are four categories of organizations that can potentially partner to leverage additional contributions and achieve scalable and sustainable ICT4D solutions:

- **Technology providers** supply hardware, software, communications, and technology support services for one or more components of ICT4D solutions (note that these can be at a global, country, or local community level depending on the context).
- **Nonprofit organizations** focus on using these solutions in the field; some of these can be consortiums, like NetHope or the mHealth Alliance, that use scale to reduce ICT4D costs and risks and accelerate learning across their membership.
- **Donors** have a particular interest in the benefits and use of ICT4D in field programming to deliver more innovative, impactful, and **sustainable** ways of applying their limited resources.
- A range of **private sector** organizations and other institutions (note that these can be at a global, country, or local community level depending on the context) bring their day-to-day products, services, and experiences to bear in support of long-term, large-scale solutions.

For INGOs to be successful, they need to look at partnering in new and innovative ways. This could mean working with new kinds of partners, which may be uncomfortable at first. It may also mean changing the nature of the partnership and the skills and competencies applied, compared to conventional programs.

Planning Considerations
A successful ICT4D program starts with good planning. This includes recognizing up front that the program will use technology and factoring it into the grant application and early planning efforts. When one is planning to include ICT in a program, it is important to consider the financial and human resource impacts of the following:

- the hardware (mobiles, laptops, etc.),
- the software (the applications that will run on the hardware),
- the servers and data management solutions (Are these managed by the INGO, or are they software-as-a-service solutions?),
- time and skills required to customize the hardware and software to meet the needs of the program,
- the training time required to teach staff and/or partners how to use the hardware and the software,

- the training time required to teach staff and/or partners about how to use the applications and the importance of capturing quality information,
- the maintenance of the hardware and software (Can this be done by the INGO's IT organization, or are new partners required at a local program level?),
- ongoing IT and training updates over the life of the program and beyond if necessary, and
- what happens at the end of the grant cycle (Does the need that the ICT solution is supporting end, or should the program be designed so that the ICT remains in the hands of local partners or others who will continue to carry out the function of the program?).

Clearly, having a broad understanding of the need that ICT is going to support will ensure that you select a right-sized ICT solution for the program. For example, in the case of remote data collection with a five-question survey, it is possible to use a very basic mobile handset with a survey form application. However, for complex communications and training, it might be necessary to use a laptop with customized training courses.

Planning and budgeting for these elements in advance goes a long way toward ensuring a sustainable and successful ICT4D program. Don't underestimate the change in management activities required to train users, especially if upgrades to the technology will occur over the life cycle of the program.

4.4. ICT as a "Disruptive" Technology for Established International NGOs

In the *The Innovator's Dilemma*,[13] published in 1997, Clayton Christensen makes an interesting distinction between sustaining technologies, which help incumbents to continuously improve, and disruptive technologies, which can ultimately lead to the failure of even the strongest incumbents, despite, it seems, their best efforts to continuously improve their products and their cost competiveness and to listen carefully to the needs of their customers.

He goes on to explore if it is possible for the most talented and hardworking executives of successful, well-established organizations to simultaneously do what is right for their near-term health and still focus adequate resources on the disruptive technologies that ultimately could lead to their downfall.

In his research, Christensen makes use of some great examples from the computer disk storage PC and earth-moving industries, among others, where large, established, and, in most cases, very well-managed businesses gradually lost market share because they failed to address disruptive technologies in their respective sectors. Since his initial research was published, the list of examples has grown.

Examples Where Disruptive Technology Caused the Demise of Established Incumbents

An interesting example is Ryanair, which has grown at an astonishing pace since the early nineties. How did this large and very profitable low-cost airline come from nowhere to become, by 2009, greater in both passenger numbers and market capitalization than British Airlines, Lufthansa, and Air France?[14] Each of these established airlines had a long and proud reputation, a tremendously strong brand, with privileged access to the largest and most strategic airports, plus a network of relationships with the major airlines across the world.

How did Amazon.com, a company only founded in 1995, develop by 2003 a market capitalization of more than ten times the value of Barnes & Noble?[15] The latter had been in business for almost a century and had tremendous experience, a trusted brand, an enormous back catalog, and over 50,000 knowledgeable and dedicated staff. How could they be usurped in a short few years by an absolute newcomer?

Why did the major international telecom players such as BT, AT&T, and Deutsche Telekom, with established monopoly positions in all of the major markets, with tremendous resources, have such a mixed bag of fortunes in the mobile telephony and broadband Internet market, allowing Vodafone, Orange, and others to emerge and take center stage?

How did BlackBerry from a standing start or Apple from a position of relative weakness come to be the dominant players in smart handsets, usurping the likes of Hewlett-Packard, Motorola, Nokia, and others?

Why Do Incumbents Fail to Deal With Disruptive Technology Changes?

Part of the answers to this curious question can be attributed to the ideas and insights Christensen identified through the concept of disruptive technologies. Disruptive technologies somehow change the nature of competition, and change it in a way that large successful and well-established incumbents fail, for whatever reason, to address. The underlying question in each case is why such apparently well-managed companies, who clearly tried their best to be as close and responsive to their customers as possible and had tremendous market positioning, great brands, huge resources, and great trust with a long-established customer base, could be usurped over a relatively short period by firms that came from virtually nowhere.

The analysis and observations in the *The Innovator's Dilemma* provide some very interesting insights that cast light on why large successful incumbents tend, in the early days, to pass over or even stay clear of new products and services based on disruptive technology. Why is this the case? There are a number of interesting factors why the kinds of products that emerge through disruptive technologies are not enormously attractive to established incumbents or indeed to most of their customers. For example:

1. On the basis of conventional measures, the **price/performance levels of the products from the disruptive technology initially underperform the established expectations** of the vast majority of the existing customer base, hence they do not actively demand these new products or services.
2. The **segment of customers who prefer the new product or service is initially small in scale**, and hence the attractiveness of the opportunity is limited for incumbents who are accustomed to operating only at a very large scale.
3. The **markets for these new disruptive technologies are not well understood and are almost impossible to analyze, predict, and size** from the outset. Hence, it is difficult for large established incumbents to prepare investment cases based on conventional requirements to pursue these new opportunities.
4. On the other hand, where these new products do offer additional features and performance dimensions that go beyond what conventional products can provide, these new **attributes are not ones that large established customers can easily take advantage of** and hence do not value.
5. Surprisingly, the new products prompted by disruptive technology are often simpler and **created through established components that can be bought off the shelf** and, in most cases, are not dependent on leading-edge restricted technologies. This is challenging and uncomfortable for established incumbents who have **made a significant cumulative investment in their own proprietary technologies and methods.**

Sustaining Technology Versus Disruptive Technology

"What all sustaining technologies have in common is that they improve the performance of established products, along the dimensions of performance that mainstream customers in major markets have historically valued. Most technological advances in a given industry are sustaining in character."

"Occasionally, however, disruptive technologies emerge: innovations that result in worse product performance, at least in the near-term. Ironically, in each of the instances studied, it was disruptive technology that precipitated the leading firms' failure."

Disruptive Technologies Versus Rational Investments

"First, disruptive products are simpler and cheaper; they generally promise lower margins, not greater profits. Second, disruptive technologies typically are first commercialized in emerging or insignificant markets. And third, leading firms' most profitable customers generally don't want, and indeed initially can't use, products based on disruptive technologies."

Source. Clayton M. Christensen, *The Innovator's Dilemma,* pp. xv, xvii.

Hence, it is not entirely surprising that large, established, and successful incumbents are slow to embrace these new opportunities. However, there are a number of additional barriers that can stand in the way.

6. At the early stages, **management and staff do not have the skills or familiarity with the new technology** the disruptive technology demands and hence tend to pass on small introductory opportunities. The more they ignore these opportunities, and others gain experience, the less well equipped they feel as time goes by.

7. The structure and organizational **decision-making procedures are poorly equipped to deal with the nature of these new kinds of opportunities** that may not fall into the normal familiar pattern in respect to approvals and decision making.

8. And finally, the most difficult challenge for even the most talented managers is that large established **incumbents are often locked into a familiar and comfortable "value network" in terms of external relationships with customers, suppliers, and other partners,** as well as locked into assumptions around margins and levels of cost and overhead.

Hence, not only is it just the internal issues around skills, experience, and decision making that stand in the way, it is also the network of external relationships and assumptions. The products implied by a disruptive technology potentially map onto a very different value network of relationships and assumptions.

Are ICT and Related Trends Disruptive Technologies for International NGOs?

As demonstrated in the previous sections, the wealth of possibilities and opportunities generated through ICT can be regarded as a tremendous chance to further strengthen and expand what INGOs are seeking to achieve through their programs. That is the "glass half full" scenario and has been the broad flavor of our analysis in sections 4.2 and 4.3. Hence, in Christensen's terms, we have implicitly treated these emerging ICT possibilities as sustaining technologies, meaning that large successful INGOs will be able to rise to the challenge and continue to enhance and develop their programs, taking full advantage of the new ICT possibilities.

However, there is an alternative "glass half empty" scenario. In this situation we have to question if large INGOs are able to adapt to embrace the range of ICT and related opportunities driven not just by the wave of the new ICT possibilities but also by the other international economic, trade, and political developments that accompany these changes. If we apply the Christensen distinction, it would suggest that new entities and organizations could gradually take root and push aside the big INGOs we know today.

Which of these scenarios is the most valid? Can INGOs evolve and adapt to remain center stage in the war against poverty, or will they gradually be marginalized by other entities, combinations, and contributions because, like many other large and established incumbents in other sectors, they are unable to respond to the disruptive technologies that emerge, despite their very best efforts? In addressing the question we will look at two veins of thought.

Comparing ICT Possibilities in Development With the Characteristics of Disruptive Technologies

First, if we examine new possibilities and opportunities being brought to bear by ICT and associated developments and compare them to the attributes of disruptive technology as summarized in items 1 to 5 above, what we can observe, and what parallels can we draw? In summary, we can see the following:

- The cost/performance metrics of new innovative ICT programs may align with a set of measures different from those that are traditionally used in the design and assessment of field programs. In addition, the new possibilities offer considerable features and benefits that may not be easily recognized and valued. **Hence it is difficult for staff in the field to assess and put forward confident business cases and funding proposals using traditional approaches.**

- The scale of the ICT opportunities embraced by large incumbent INGOs has, so far, been small. As indicated earlier, the use of ICT in development programs supported by INGOs has been **relatively ad hoc with many pilots but very few large-scale, sustainable examples.**

- Although donors are starting to embrace the benefits of ICT and provide financing, it is still on a small scale as **the market for the use of ICT4D is not yet fully understood.**

In relation to incumbent INGO capability and positioning (items 6 to 8 above), there are a number of additional challenges:

- Many incumbent **INGOs are not well equipped** to be able to support and nurture the effective exploitation of ICT for the benefit of development. They simply do not have the skills, knowledge, and expertise at either an individual level or an organizational level, and they don't have the reach to adequately scale and support ICT solutions once they are implemented.

- INGOs have strong ongoing **momentum in terms of their current structures, staffing, and ways of operating.** It is relatively easy to utilize ICT to sustain and improve the current INGO organizational construct and approaches, making useful but incremental progress. It is incredibly difficult to be able to conceive of new ways of working that are fundamentally different from the status quo, with different ideas around approach, strategy, competence, skills, and organizational models. Bridging the gap between INGO IT staff and program staff is a big challenge for many organizations.

- And finally, large, established, incumbent NGOs are often **locked into a familiar and comfortable "value network" in terms of relationships with donors, partners, beneficiaries, and local stakeholders**, as well as assumptions around cost ratios and levels of overhead. The visionary programs facilitated by ICT as a disruptive technology potentially maps onto a very different value network of relationships and assumptions.

In summary, we can observe that many of the characteristics and barriers indicated above do resonate loud and clear and also link very closely with the challenges set out in the introduction to this chapter.

Indirect Impacts of ICT and Related Developments on the Raison D'être of International NGOs

We can take the impact of this "disruptive" technology and associated trends one step further. Clearly, the evolution of ICT and its related possibilities over the past few decades has made the world feel like a much smaller place. So what are some of the more indirect impacts of these developments on the poor in the developing world, on the world at large in which INGOs operate, and particularly on the raison d'être of INGOs?

We isolated six important gaps in table 4.1, which have been important drivers for the work of INGOs over the past fifty-plus years. These include the following:

- Information and understanding gaps
- Communications gap
- Access gap
- Resources gap
- Trade gap
- Rights and governance gap

If we review and challenge the key assumptions or foundation stones on which INGOs were founded, it is possible to see that the important changes facilitated by ICT are affecting the basis of these assumptions. Some of these assumptions are still clearly valid today, but arguably a number are becoming less important and less relevant as the decades go by. These are examined (somewhat provocatively) in table 4.1.

4.5. Conclusions and Recommendations

What are we to conclude from this analysis? If you are an executive in a large established INGO, trying to do your very best to help the poor and disadvantaged within your current constructs, should you throw your hands in the air and just wait for inevitable decline? We believe not.

In summary, there is a raft of opportunities presented by new ICT possibilities. Some of these provide incremental improvements and effectiveness either to existing programs or to improve the performance of INGOs. This

Table 4.1

Challenging the Gaps and Assumptions on the Role of International NGOs

Gap	Historic Mind-set	Emerging Reality
Information and understanding gaps	INGOs enable the understanding of the real needs and context of the people in poverty in the developing world.	With an increasingly connected global media, Internet and social network channels, the role of INGOs in this space is less compelling than in the past.
Communications gap	INGOs facilitate communication between the rich in the affluent North and the poor communities and other beneficiaries in developing countries (the South).	The penetration of mobile technologies and the Internet, coupled with social media access, is accelerating everywhere. Consequently there is an increasing number of ways that North–South and South–South communications can occur without the traditional INGO facilitation.
Access gap	INGOs are trusted intermediaries that provide direct assistance to the poor and disadvantaged in developing countries.	Trend toward donors going directly to local NGO partners. Also there is a shift in thinking around good development practice is deemphasizing direct local service provision as a way of helping those in need.
Resources gap	INGOs are a conduit to help address the big resource gap between the North and the South.	The North and South delineation has less and less meaning as many new sources of trade and influence, not just China, Brazil, and India but also a raft of other developing economies such as Mexico, Indonesia, and Korea, are becoming much more important. In addition, many developing countries are rich in scarce natural resources such as oil and precious metals (e.g., South Africa, Namibia, Nigeria, Sudan, Ghana, Angola, Uganda, etc.).
Trade gap	Countries in the developing world have low relevance and connection to international trade and so have little capacity to sell or little capacity to buy.	This is no longer true. Developing countries are emerging as a key part of the future growth of the global economy and are high on the agenda for many international companies, providing new growing customer markets as suppliers of goods and raw materials and as locations to produce and manufacture goods and services.
Rights and governance gap	NGOs have a central role in highlighting breaches in human rights and undemocratic practices.	Recent events have shown that the Internet, global media, and related channels provide many rapid channels to expose issues.

is the right-hand side of the diagram in figure 4.5. However, on the left side of this diagram, there are also many opportunities that have the potential to transform the development sector and hence imply much more radical change to the shape and contribution of INGOs.

To conclude, we would like to set out the following two broad recommendations.

Embrace the Possibilities and Strengthen Your Organization to Embrace Sustaining Technologies

1. Many of the ideas and possibilities in section 4.2 are hugely valuable sustaining technologies that can improve the scale, reach, effectiveness, and cost efficiency of programs.

2. Yes, they will require new skills, new kinds of suppliers and partners, and new organizational capacity to be able to embrace what is possible. INGOs need to embrace these new ideas, appreciating that there will be a strong learning curve at individual and organizational levels, as well as considerable discovery and learning for the other stakeholders and beneficiaries.

Invest in awareness and new skills at local and central nodes of the organization to help everyone understand the successes, the learning, and what is required to make ICT-enabled programs work at scale.

3. In addition, recognize that you will need to work alongside a different set of partners, who can contribute particular aspects of the new programs, many of whom you will not have worked with in the past. If you have, it is more likely to have been in a different capacity, in some cases as traditional donors to your programs. Leverage existing associations like NetHope and the mHealth Alliance to reduce the individual risk to your organization and to seek opportunities to scale and to learn from others who have done it or are currently doing it.

4. Use the new possibilities and challenges to review and refine or redesign the organization's structure and operating practices. In particular, for organizations with an organization based on the simple geographical reporting structural form, this may be a time to consider a more sophisticated matrix-type organizational model. As you do this, it is also necessary to consider the changes in leadership style, as well as the rigor of management processes that are important complementary ingredients to making such a progression.

5. All of this will change the perception and status of ICT in your organization from a back office administrative support tool to something that is integral to high-impact programming. To facilitate this, it is likely that you will need a chief information officer who is fully integrated into the top execu-

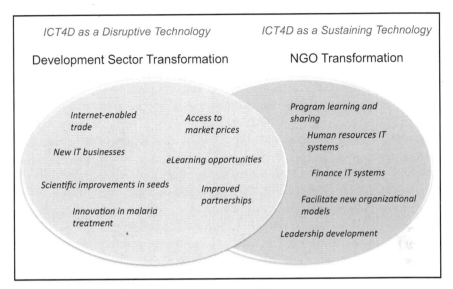

Figure 4.5 ICT transformation of development and NGOs.

tive team, who can confidently embed ICT into the development process, and who is willing and able to spearhead these new opportunities for the organization. One likely development over the next ten years is the transformation of development approaches through new ICT possibilities, interlinked with a transformation of internal NGO capability.

Linked closely with point 5 is the growing need for business analyst skills within the INGO. People who can understand programs but also have an appreciation for ICT and the ability to translate program impact requirements into ICT solutions. People who are also able to see the importance of developing ICT solutions that can be leveraged across multiple programs in multiple locations rather than customized for a single project or program. Building connections between IT staff and program staff is a critical step to ensure effective design and implementation of impactful programs with an ICT component.

Be Ready and Willing to Recognize Disruptive Technologies for What They Are

Where there are opportunities driven by disruptive technologies, recognize them for what they are. They may not match well with the skills, capabilities, and management approaches of your existing organization. In fact, these opportunities may in some cases replace and cannibalize what you currently do.

They may initially be small in scale, be difficult to predict and analyze, require iterative trials and much discovery and learning, and require very new sets of skills and organizational mentoring. Also, they may be part of a value network somewhat different from that of the conventional programs of an INGO.

1. Recognize these opportunities for what they are and, if necessary, be prepared to put in place and fund a different organizational entity, most likely as a separate unit, using an arm's-length arrangement. This should be unconstrained by the rules, assumptions, and current ways of working and be resourced with skills, expertise, and leadership that is better matched to that opportunity.

2. Be ready to let this new entity evolve, grow, and compete with the legacy organization. This will inevitably create considerable internal tensions. However, it will give the organization the best chance of pursuing the value of this opportunity for the benefit of the poor. In addition, it will also promote much more learning and stretch than trying to incubate these new kinds of opportunities within the current organizational model.

3. Put in place some clear and tailored achievement or progress points specific to that new entity, to ensure that if the direction and assumptions were not valid, and success is unlikely, you know when to pull the plug or change the construct of the idea to one that has a chance of succeeding.

4. Alternatively, if the new initiative achieves success, matures, and reaches material scale, once the learning and new programs are robust, do not be afraid to bring the new entity back closer to the legacy organization, even reintegrating when the time is right.

5. Be careful to take a balanced approach to bottom-up and top-down opportunities. Establishing grand, global partnerships with big-name technology firms or other large organizations may be more of a recipe for wasting scarce time and resources than producing new worthwhile ideas. Most often, ideas and possibilities emerging from the field are the best sources of new prospects as they are real, are well grounded in the needs of the poor, and have the support of the local staff who ultimately need to make them happen. However, establishing pragmatic partnerships with the appropriate organizations will be useful and necessary to extend the reach and to scale the opportunities to make a material difference to the lives of the poor.

Additional Lessons and Guidance

To emphasize, at an overall leadership level, it is very important to create the organizational context in terms of understanding, support, and management disciplines, as well as to develop a focused network of relationships with other essential organizations. This will offer the best chance of identifying the "gems" and is less likely to waste time on initiatives that have little or no chance of success. The following are points to remember.

1. What is important is to use ICT to support the achievement of program objectives; it is not using ICT for the sake of ICT.

2. It is unlikely that there is one single perfect solution. Do not aim to build a perfect solution for a single program; instead apply an 80/20 approach, with the wider goal being that the solution can be sustainable and scaled within the existing program, across other similar programs and across geographies.

3. Try to plan for ICT, especially the end state support, right from the start. ICT without adequate training and support won't succeed. Plan how to support, sustain, and scale from day one.

4. Break down internal silos and build energy and excitement around ICT in development programs across program staff and IT staff, across headquarters, regions, and countries.

5. Look at innovative ways of partnering, especially with technology organizations as strategic partners.

Finally, we acknowledge that ICT programs can and do go wrong, and it is an even greater failure to not reflect and learn from your experiences. However, we believe that ICT4D presents an enormous chance for INGOs to multiply their contribution and provide a springboard to unprecedented levels of impact.

Notes

1. UN International Telecommunication Union, "Measuring the Information Society Report 2010," February 23, 2010, http://www.itu.int/ITU-D/ict/publications/idi/2010/index .html.

2. Clayton M. Christensen, *The Innovator's Dilemma: When New Technologies Cause Great Firms to Fail* (Boston, MA: Harvard Business School Press, 1997).

3. UN International Telecommunication Union, "Measuring the Information Society Report 2010."

4. UN News Centre, "Communications Prices Falling Worldwide, UN Reports," February 23, 2010.

5. UN International Telecommunication Union, "Measuring the Information Society Report 2010," p. 4.

6. Vital Wave Consulting, *mHealth for Development: The Opportunity of Mobile Technology for Healthcare in the Developing World* (Washington, DC, and Berkshire, UK: UN Foundation-Vodafone Foundation Partnership, 2009).

7. Catholic Relief Services, "CRS Announces $21.8 Million Grant From Gates Foundation to Help Small-Scale African Farmers Protect Cassava From Disease," http://www.crs.org/news

room/releases/release.cfm?id=1453; http://crs.org/donate/foundations-and-corporations/intel-cor poration.cfm.

8. Jeffrey A. Hoffman, Janice R. Cunningham, Andrew J. Suleh, Aaron Sundsmo, Debra Dekker, Fred Vago, Kelly Munly, Emmy Kageha Igonya, and Jonathan Hunt-Glassman, "Mobile Direct Observation Treatment for Tuberculosis Patients: A Technical Feasibility Pilot Using Mobile Phones in Nairobi, Kenya," *American Journal of Preventative Medicine* 39, no. 1 (2010): 78–80.

9. Vital Wave Consulting, *mHealth for Development*, p. 5.

10. NetHope, http://hub.nethope.org/tag/mobile-health-platform/, http://www.nethope .org/media/article/the-promise-of-mobile-technology/.

11. World Economic Forum, *Amplifying the Impact: Examining the Intersection of Mobile Health and Mobile Finance; A Discussion Guide for Collaborative Insight Presented by the World Economic Forum, in Partnership With the mHealth Alliance*, p. 1, http://www3.weforum.org/ docs/WEF_HE_IntersectionMobileHealthMobileFinance_Report_2011.pdf and the Mobile Financial Services Development Report, December 2011, http://www3.weforum.org/docs/ WEF_MFSD_Report_2011.pdf.

12. Vital Wave Consulting, *mHealth for Development*, p. 25.

13. Christensen, *The Innovator's Dilemma*.

14. *The Sunday Times*, June 3, 2009.

15. Forbes.com, "Amazon Versus Barnes and Noble," August 2003.

5

Strategic Planning for International NGOs

Reflections and Perspectives

Abstract

Conducting a global strategic review is a very sensitive and demanding activity for large international NGOs. The nature of the work of these agencies, along with their complex governance and decision-making structures, can present considerable challenges. There are a number of pitfalls to navigate. The prize is great, however, in terms of achieving greater organizational alignment, cohesion, and ultimate impact. The resulting strategy should set the direction, focus, and priorities of the organization for the next five to ten years.

This chapter is a set of perspectives and reflections intended to help international NGOs (INGOs) get the most out of a strategic planning process and avoid some of the more common attendant hazards. We believe strongly that a thorough and decisive strategic planning process is a very good opportunity to address some of the issues and ideas already covered, providing a chance to make sure that the whole of the international agency is indeed greater than the sum of the parts.

We begin by setting out some of the important similarities and differences between conducting a strategic review in the development and humanitarian sectors and doing similar exercises in private sector organizations. This is followed by some reflections on what strategic planning is for, and, importantly, how a strategic review, typically carried out every five or so years, fits into the ongoing management and planning processes for any well-run global agency. It is important to emphasize that a new strategic plan should build on the progress and successes of the past and is respectful of the existing vision, mission, and values, as well as goals. In this section we also describe the typical ways by which the decisions and directions, agreed on during a strategic review, get implemented in practice.

The chapter goes on to describe some of the characteristics of a good strategic plan for any large international agency. We offer twelve specific success criteria. These are based on the author's extensive experience of strategic reviews in the private sector, as well as hands-on support of strategic reviews at a number of large international development and relief agencies.

One possible approach is set out as an illustration, though we fully acknowledge there are many possible approaches and variations in terms of how to design the process in detail. We explore some variations on that sample approach, as well as their associated pros and cons. However, the optimum process should always be carefully designed for an individual organizational context. The chapter concludes with some very practical perspectives on some frequently asked questions.

5.1. Introduction

Forward planning can be a challenging process for large international development and relief agencies. With numerous areas of need, as well as myriad new program approaches and interventions, these organizations have a multitude of options in terms of applying their scarce resources.

A good strategic planning process can be challenging, engaging, and energizing. It is truly satisfying when the process works well, as it provides the opportunity for very different views, beliefs, and assumptions to be discussed, enriched, and realigned. The process should allow an agency to gain insight into the most important external trends, innovations, and opportunities. Furthermore, the dialogue and analysis make it possible to identify and address some of the most critical strategic choices for the future, setting a direction, priorities, and goals and gaining alignment across all of the main constituents of the organization on the way ahead.

Yet even when a strategic review delivers a positive experience, it is highly unlikely that either the process or the final result will satisfy all of the people all of the time. INGOs have a cadre of management and staff at all levels who all feel they have valid and useful perspectives and have a right to be consulted. This can be an opportunity but also somewhat of a challenge.

Getting the process right is paramount. A poorly designed process will do little more than expose and emphasize deep divisions across the organization, limiting achievement of material benefits. Some organizations can be tempted to sidestep this challenge, fearing that the effort and pain of a robust strategic review is too great. Instead, they take the approach of locking a few bright people in a room and letting them write a carefully crafted plan, one that has the right language and nuance, such that nobody will object too much. As a result, the organization avoids the difficult choices, fudges the internal contradictions, and completely misses the opportunity to steer the organization onto a better course.

Unfortunately, it is sometimes possible to produce a plan that seems to be, to both the initiated and external stakeholders, a very reasonable explanation of what the organization is there to do and where it is heading but misses the real value that a robust strategic review can provide.

Common Features of Any Strategic Planning Processes

In many ways the process of conducting a strategic planning review at an INGO is similar to that employed for any organization in the private sector.

The underlying steps are pretty straightforward. Typically, during the course of a strategic review, the work needs to do the following:

1. assess the current organization's context, strengths and weaknesses, and strategic positioning
2. review the external environment, key stakeholder trends, and implications
3. identify the most important strategic issues or areas that need to be tackled
4. carry out the necessary analysis, debate, and consideration of the key issues to narrow down choices
5. make a coherent set of choices for the future
6. articulate the choices into a set of clear goals and targets to guide the organization into the future
7. identify the critical initiatives that need to be put in place to change course from business as usual, if needed, and do the business planning for the different units of the organizations in order to reset business objectives and targets in line with new strategic direction and priorities

Important Considerations or Differences for International NGOs

There are, however, some important differences in how these steps need to get carried out for large international NGOs.

First, international organizations in the private sector are increasingly tending to carry out more regular and dynamic approaches to strategic planning. However, because of the complexity of governance arrangements and considerable breadth of activities of many INGOs, **a strategic planning process may be an exceptional one-off opportunity for serious, joined-up dialogue and decision making, bringing together all of the constituents of the organization at operational, executive, and board levels.** Issues that are not tackled during a strategic review are unlikely to be properly explored for several more years. This has a number of specific implications, most notably a heightened increase in tension to ensure that the most important issues are properly addressed within the scope of the review.

Second, the nature of **the work of development agencies emphasizes consultation, engagement, and participation.** This is a key principle to take into account in the design of a strategic planning process. However, broad consultation and consensus-based decision making can sometimes be overemphasized. Proper and genuine consultation at the appropriate time and at the appropriate level can be very useful, but it needs to be very carefully carried out to be practical and meaningful rather than merely symbolic. In addition, it is important to keep a reasonable balance between effective and useful consultation on the one hand and not being overly intrusive on the day-to-day focus of the staff across the agency on the other hand.

Third, there is an unusual aspect of international development agencies, because **those who provide the funding are typically different from and in a different part of the world than the end beneficiaries.** This means that there is the possibility of an inbuilt disconnect between the perspectives and demands of those who are providing the funding and the views of development professionals on the ground in terms of what kinds of programs contribute most in the longer term. Obtaining a balanced and proportional set of views and inputs is therefore critical to accurately inform the analysis and recommendations.

The fourth key difference is that many large international development agencies typically have **an extraordinarily wide geographical footprint and scope of activities compared to private sector organizations.** Larger INGOs such as World Vision, CARE International, or Plan International may cover anything from fifty to one hundred or more countries across multiple continents and span a broad range of domains such as relief, health, agriculture, microfinance, governance, and inclusion. **This stretch or fragmentation of interests and outputs can leave the coordinating processes and systems of these INGOs relatively weak.** This is very understandable, especially since there are not sufficient economies of scale to justify the substantial system-level investments that would be required to integrate and strengthen the organization's collective enabling processes across the world. A strategic review offers a once-off opportunity to bring together, at least at a point in time, the knowledge, information, and perspectives of the many constituents of the organization to inform the future strategic direction and priorities.

Last, but by no means least, **international NGOs have a constant challenge to justify their legitimacy.** The work that they do is continuously questioned in terms of its efficiency, impact, and longer-term sustainability. Indeed, there are regular commentators in the popular media that claim that the work that is done by these agencies is of limited value and impact, if not counterproductive. It is critical that international NGOs are robust and deliberate in their approach to strengthening their legitimacy as part of their strategic planning efforts.

This is likely to involve some thoughtful (and sometimes sensitive) discussion and alignment on the agency's *theory of change*, that is, its collective understanding of how positive and lasting social and economic progress can best be achieved in poor communities and countries. This should lead to an improved understanding and definition of what that agency's specific role and contribution will be within that theory of change. This should in turn lead to a clear definition of what the agency is and needs to really excel at, which we term "core competence." The challenge of defining core competencies is the subject of chapter 2.

5.2. Connecting a Strategic Plan With Ongoing Planning and Management of the Agency

Before discussing the characteristics of a good strategic review, it is worth taking a step back and reflecting on how a strategic review fits into the ongoing planning and management activities for an INGO.

Too often, strategic reviews can be accused of becoming an island of analysis, debate, and decisions and not being sufficiently connected to the previous progress, direction, and momentum of an organization. This is not to imply that a strategic review cannot or should not result in a change of direction or focus. Clearly, this may well be required. However, it should build on what is already in place where at all possible. This means that it is more likely to review and refine external goals and business objectives, not invent a totally new set goals and definitions. It might challenge and potentially refine the agency's mission, vision, and values, but in many cases these will not be altered materially as a result of a strategic review.

The diagram set out in figure 5.1 is one of the most important illustrations in this chapter, as it positions a strategic review as a one-off exercise, typically conducted every five or so years (right-hand side of the diagram), in the context of the ongoing components of a planning and management framework of any large international agency.

Commenting briefly on this diagram, let us start with the left-hand part, that is, the components of the ongoing planning and management framework, elements of which would be found in any INGO, at any time.

Ongoing Components of an Agency's Planning and Management Framework

At the top, all agencies will have some statements that define the following:

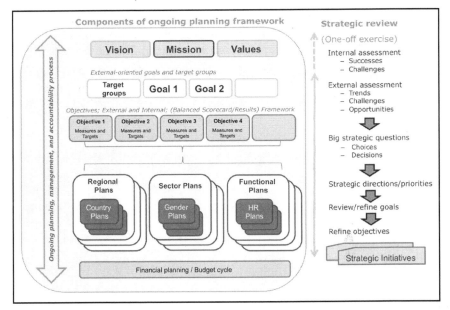

Figure 5.1 Strategic reviews and the ongoing planning framework.

- **Vision**, often defined as how the agency believes the world should ideally be, for example, a world without poverty and injustice;
- **Mission**, the specific aim or purpose of this agency toward achieving that vision; and
- **Values**, the beliefs or principles that the organization holds dear and guides how it goes about its work.

Underneath these, driven by the mission, is a **set of goals** that are typically externally facing. These goals define what the organization is seeking to contribute over the next number of years in terms of targeted changes, and progress in relation to issues of poverty and injustice. At this level, there is often a definition of the target groups that the agency is seeking to particularly focus on in the pursuit of its mission.

These externally oriented goals are often translated into a set of more **concrete objectives**, which are likely to be a mix of externally facing objectives that are a more specific definition of the external goals, as well as some very important internally oriented goals, for example, concerning the organizational capability, capacity, reach, or reputation. A good way of thinking of this mix is through the ideas in the "balanced scorecard" approach that has become well accepted in the private sector.[1] This topic is discussed further in chapter 6. Much has been written about lessons and techniques in the implementation of this idea, including for the not-for-profit sector. A good example is the book by Paul Niven titled *Balanced Scorecard for Government and Nonprofit Agencies.*[2]

All of these objectives should ideally be translated into meaningful **measures with associated targets**, which could be set for one-, three-, or five-year horizons as appropriate. In turn, these objectives and targets for the totality of the organization should be aligned with **local plans at regional, country, sector, or functional levels** and, of course, aligned with departmental plans and individual objectives as part of the individual performance management process. Finally, all of these plans should align directly with the financial planning and budgeting cycle as indicated in the lower part of figure 5.1. This alignment is often a challenge and requires considerable tenacity because of the complex legal and governance structures that sometimes exist in terms of affiliates and entities and also when different parts of the organization do not have even a common financial year.

Finally, we would like to draw your attention to the vertical arrow on the left of the chart called "Ongoing planning, management, and accountability process." This is too often a weak link for international agencies and is often not very effective or is in some cases nonexistent. We touched on this explicitly in chapter 1 and also discuss it in more detail in chapter 6. It is this process that can, if it operates effectively, ensure that the overall goals and objectives at an organizational level are useful and practical. Importantly it also connects the strategic externally facing goals with the objectives, measures, and targets throughout the organization. This is a critical part of the organizational glue to ensure that the focus, goals, objectives, and ongoing progress of the entire organization are aligned.

How a Strategic Review, as a One-Off Exercise, Links With the Ongoing Planning Framework

In the course of carrying out a strategic review, typically a one-off exercise, a refresh and update to the left part of the diagram in figure 5.1 would be expected. Starting at the higher levels in that figure, the strategic review would put in place a foundation for the subsequent refreshment of plans at country, sector, and functional levels. In doing this, it is important to emphasize the fine balance between continuity and consistency on the one hand and changes and refinements that are deemed to be essential to steer the entire organization on a better course in the pursuit of its mission on the other.

First, the three top-level components (Vision, Mission, and Values) are typically discussed and reviewed at some level during the course of a strategic review but more often remain fairly consistent throughout multiple strategic planning periods. However, in the course of a strategic review, it is likely that these externally facing goals and underlying objectives will come under considerable scrutiny and will often be refined or changed, because previous goals have already been met or have been found to be unhelpful or because new learning or insight indicates there are more effective goals or objectives that will better guide the organization into the future. However, it is important to keep as much continuity as possible in terms of definitions to avoid confusion and to maintain momentum where at all possible.

How Do Recommendations and Directions Get Implemented in Reality?

It is important to clarify, up front, how the recommendations and decisions made during a strategic review are likely to get implemented. The short answer is through an implementation plan; however, there are three main ways this comes about:

1. Implementation is effected **through an update or refinement of the goals and objectives framework for the entire organization.** This should in turn guide management decisions and priorities in the years ahead.
2. These revised goals and objectives get translated across all components of the organization **through an update of country, domain, and functional plans.** These new plans then inform the allocation of funds and financial plans through the budgeting process.
3. **One-off initiatives** are utilized to put in place the decisions, directions, and changes that are implied by the new strategic plan, where the way forward cannot be delivered by routes one and two or needs special investment and effort to deliver the changes desired within an acceptable time frame.

Strategic Planning as Part of an Ongoing Process

Finally, it is worth emphasizing that while a strategic review is a very significant event in the direction setting for an INGO, in reality strategic planning and reflection is part of an ongoing process for all organizations, with a

Strategic planning is more than a one-and-done exercise. It can help senior leadership continuously understand and optimize the organization's needs and opportunities.

Strategic Planning
- Set priorities
- Establish alignment and direction

Operational Planning
- Target setting
- Budgeting

External Environment Analysis

Ongoing Improvement
- Program analysis
- Program impacts
- Evaluation of priorities

Progress Evaluation
- Regular updates and reporting
- Changing priorities

Figure 5.2 Strategic planning as part of an ongoing process.

continuous cycle of strategic planning, operational planning, progress evaluation, and ongoing improvement. This cycle is illustrated in figure 5.2. This effort is a central part of the ongoing role of all senior executives.

5.3. A Good Strategic Plan: Are We There Yet?

Given the particular context and challenges of strategic planning in this sector, and the important differences outlined earlier, it is worth standing back and asking the question, **What are some of the important characteristics of a good strategic plan in this sector?** In addition, when teams enter the latter stages of a robust strategic planning process, it is reasonable to ask, **Are we there yet? When will we be there?** The following pointers provide some answers to these questions and are intended to help guide your thinking as you design the specific process relevant to your particular organizational context. The following are, in our view, **some of the more important attributes of a good strategic review** for INGOs.

The Basics
1. **It brings longer-term clarity in terms of the direction and priorities of the organization,** helping define what it is seeking to achieve, what it plans

---

Strategic Review: Success Criteria

The Basics
1. Clarity in direction and priorities; describes a future vision for the agency that is unifying, stretching, and inspiring
2. Addresses important strategic issues or choices
3. Provides guidance on prioritizing investment opportunities
4. Stipulates clear, high-level calibration goals and milestones
5. Is embraced and approved by governance boards

The Heart
6. Brings the organization together intellectually and emotionally
7. Tests and strengthens the organization's theory of change
8. Increases confidence in its own role and legitimacy
9. Brings increased clarity of core competencies

Additional Value
10. Features prominently in the life of the organization and is a valuable communication tool for all staff
11. Helps external stakeholders understand what the organization does
12. Provides an anchor for planning and performance management

---

to do, and, equally important, what activities or programs it does not intend to participate in (because, for example, they can best be done by others or the benefits of certain approaches are unproven). In doing this, **it should describe a future vision for the agency, which is unifying, "stretching," and inspiring for the entire workforce.**

2. **It should provide guidance or, in some cases, answers to important strategic issues or choices** (implicit or explicit) that have emerged since the previous strategic review. These may have been provoked by internal or external challenges or perhaps new opportunities, which may well cause misalignment and tension unless adequately dealt with. A good strategic planning process should also provide guidance in relation to important issues that are expected to emerge in the coming years.

3. **It provides focus and direction when prioritizing endless lists of investment opportunities,** as well as reduces debate on ideas, initiatives, or investments that don't fit. Ideally, this clarity will become pervasive, such that the energy of the people in the organization is concentrated on ideas and innovations that fit on the strategic canvas. Hence, proposals are less likely to surface or attract much effort and cost (and generate much noise) unless they are aligned with the organization's strategic direction and priorities.

4. **It specifies some clear high-level calibration goals over the life of the plan** (typically five or more years), making it possible to track progress in the delivery of the strategy. As an aside, we believe it is very important for the plan to have early "traction" within the day-to-day life of the organization. In this regard the "half-life" principle is a useful guiding principle. This principle suggests that half of the changes implied by the new strategic plan should be put in place within the first twelve to eighteen months of the strategic horizon. Thus, if the strategic review defines some major strategic shifts or a change in direction, a good strategic plan should set out, promptly, what this means in terms of practical actions and/or changes needed to rapidly realign the organization.

However, it is important to emphasize that in some situations it is absolutely valid to have a strategy that basically says that the organization should keep its current trajectory and merely sets some stretching goals or milestones along that path.

5. **It is understood, embraced, and approved by the formal governance boards** that have a responsibility for the strategic direction of each component of the global organization. This is more easily said than done. Gaining approval can be the easiest part, particularly if boards are less aware of or less connected to the reality of organizational context and choices. Achieving "understanding" and "embracing" can be more challenging. In some cases, it may be helpful to engage representatives on key boards to collaborate in the development of the new strategy. They can bring important external perspectives and expertise and can help explain and communicate new strategic directions and goals, as well as implied changes, to their colleagues on the various boards.

The Heart

6. **It brings the organization together intellectually and emotionally**, at least at a point in time, providing a kind of glue for different parts and levels of the organization. International NGOs can sometimes have a complex network of governance structures, spanning funding and program countries with multiple boards. This is getting increasingly complex as some agencies follow the popular and well-intentioned trend toward the establishment of greater autonomy within program countries, including the creation of local boards. A well-run strategic planning process can provide a unique opportunity for all constituents of the organization to come together and seek alignment in terms of direction, creating a single set of priorities for all of the units and governance nodes of the organization.

7. **It should unpack, test, and strengthen the organization's theory of change.** Achieving genuine and deep alignment on how positive social and economic change comes about in poor communities, countries, and regions provides a strong foundation for a cohesive, high-performing development agency. In simple terms, this could be articulated as a shared understanding of the main characteristics of a good development program. Most organizations find it relatively easy to gain consensus on statements around purpose and vision and even values. However, deep alignment on the theory of change and specifically on what good development practice means in reality is often less easy. Without this, it may be difficult to make some of the important organizational choices, both during the review and in subsequent years.

Unsurprisingly, misalignments often exist between funding offices and field program functions in terms of what donors are willing to support on the one hand and what might be regarded as good development practice on the ground on the other. However, misalignment also often exists between skilled staff in the field whose views have been shaped by their own experiences and beliefs. Of course, achieving alignment should not, and need not, be to the detriment of continuously learning and gaining a better and deeper understanding of how positive change happens. In fact, it is our firm view that having a shared perspective in terms of policy and methodology provides a key foundation for ongoing learning and innovation.

8. **It should strengthen the confidence of the organization in its own legitimacy,** providing evidence to support the organization's right to act in support of the poor, for example, its right to be an effective contributor in advocacy initiatives at local, national, and international levels. In a world of increasing scrutiny in terms of efficiency, impact, and legitimacy, this is a critical item to tackle during a strategic review.

The legitimacy of large agencies is often more fragile than they would like to admit. Strengthening legitimacy is likely to include a range of factors, such as transparency and accountability to beneficiaries and to donors and partners. It may also rest on its achievement of development sector outcomes. It could also be vested in the organization's independence, as well as its technical knowledge or expertise. The topic of organizational legitimacy is usefully explored in Paul Ronalds's recent book *The Change Imperative: Creating the Next Generation NGO.*[3]

9. Building on this confidence, a good strategic plan should ideally **seek clarity on the most important core competencies that define what the organization is really good at and needs to be really good at in the future.** It should

also help the organization gain an appreciation of the underlying capabilities, new investments, and initiatives that need to be in place to strengthen its core competencies into the future. This idea is explored in more depth in chapter 2.

Additional Value

10. The final plan should be easily understood, be recognized as a key decision-steering document, and feature prominently in the daily life of the organization. While it is a physical document, the ideas and directives it contains should have "roots" and broad ownership across the organization. The launch of the strategic planning process and its execution and implementation should be designed with this in mind. Looking forward, **a good strategic plan should be an invaluable communication tool for all staff,** helping them to understand what the organization aims to achieve, as well as assisting each department and individual to better understand their efforts within the broader context of the organization's direction and goals.

11. **It should help external stakeholders understand what the organization does,** what the organization seeks to achieve, in which circumstances they might cooperate with the organization in the implementation of complementary programs. It often makes sense to have a simplified, external version of a strategic plan that is tailored to the information needs of external stakeholders.

12. **It should be the anchor for, as well as provide direction for, business planning, financial planning, and performance management processes at organizational and individual levels.** This will help ensure that the different units or constituents of an organization are working toward a common goal in a coherent and productive manner. As mentioned earlier, this is a particular challenge for many NGOs today, given the status and maturity of their international planning and management approaches. This challenge is a recurring theme across our research and is discussed in more detail in chapter 6.

5.4. Basic Elements of an Illustrative Approach

The following is an overview of some of the main components of an "illustrative" approach. This builds on the core elements of any solid strategic planning process. It feeds from what we argued is particularly different or special for strategic reviews in this sector, as set out in section 5.2, and also reflects the attributes of a good strategic plan, as set out in section 5.3.

This illustrative approach tries to find a balance between pace and focus, with a reasonable level of structured participation. This example is intended as a starter or "outline" template for international agencies contemplating such a review.

As indicated earlier, there are a number of ways of executing a strategic review. For a particular organization to have the best chance at delivering a high-quality, implementable strategy, the specific context and pressures facing it need careful consideration in the crafting of an appropriate approach.

Main Stages of Work

Figure 5.3 gives an overview of this illustrative approach with both the sequence of key activities and the indicative timings. Starting on the right footing is one of our major lessons for strategic reviews, particularly in this sector. International NGOs can sometimes be highly charged organizations, with deep-rooted beliefs and sensitivities.

In the preconsultation phase, the emphasis is on preparing the organization and setting a good foundation for a high-quality review. This will require considerable consultation with management and staff, board representatives, and also important external stakeholders and partners.

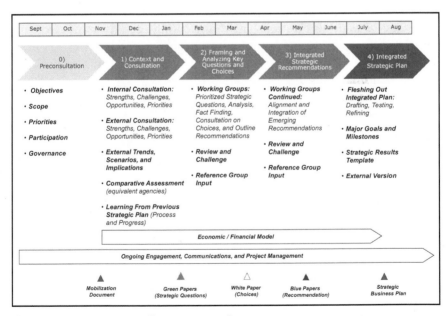

Figure 5.3 Strategic review: Illustrative approach.

It is imperative that a strategic planning process is set off in the most positive and inclusive manner possible. In other words, failure can easily and accidentally be "designed in" at the outset. What needs to be gained at this stage is an understanding of the varying perspectives; initial views on some of the key strategic questions that need to be tackled; views on participation, pace, timing, and governance; and collection of any lessons from the previous strategic planning process.

Following preconsultation, development of the strategic plan can be broken down into four main stages of work. The first three stages are dedicated to framing and analyzing key strategic questions, clarifying choices, and making recommendations. The final stage is about articulating and finessing an integrated strategic plan that communicates the direction both internally and externally, as well as defining, at a reasonable level, what needs to be done to pursue that direction.

Underpinning these stages are two ongoing activities. The first is the considerable effort that needs to be devoted to communication, engagement, and project management. This continues for the entire duration and is a very important part of any successful review. The second is to establish an integrated business and financial model of the agency, incorporating income, costs and investment, and numbers and types of donors, programs, and geographies. This will be hugely valuable in helping to assess the key trade-offs and the implications of alternative strategic recommendations as the work proceeds.

1. **Context and consultation.** This stage is essentially about understanding and analyzing the internal and external environments to identify and confirm the key strategic issues or questions that need to be tackled during the review. In this stage, the external environment in which the agency will have to operate in the next five to ten years is examined, focusing on the key trends and contextual points, their likelihood, and the impact on the stakeholders the agency serves. It also examines the internal environment within the agency, including strengths, weaknesses, priorities, and opportunities.

At this stage, where feasible, it may be useful to carry out a "lessons learned" review of the previous strategic plan. Evaluate actual progress against the goals or targets described in the previous strategic plan, understanding where progress was strong, what blockages emerged, and what further insights could drive a more successful process this time around.

This combination of activities is intended to get as broad a view as possible from every part of the organization of the critical issues and questions that staff and management in the agency feel could be considered as part of the review. This will provide the long list of strategic questions or issues that go forward to the next stage for consideration.

2. **Analyzing key strategic questions and choices.** This stage provides the cornerstones of a strategic review. It takes the long list of questions from the previous phase and stringently groups and prioritizes them. It's vital to be able to articulate why each question is particularly important to address. It is also necessary to give some careful consideration to the feasibility of addressing each issue productively at this time.

Once there is an established, clear, succinct, and prioritized list of strategic questions, it is necessary to frame each question so that it is both precise and robust. It is important to be able to articulate the key discontinuities behind the question, be they problems, challenges, or opportunities. Then frame the specific strategic question in a way that responds to these discontinuities. At this stage, it will also be helpful to hypothesize the range of choices that may be worth considering in response to this strategic question, making sure that radical thinking is encouraged.

The next step is to do a more thorough exploration and analysis of each prioritized strategic question. It is likely that some considerable data gathering, consultation, analysis, and discussion will be required to gain a deeper understanding of the key discontinuities behind the question and also to help articulate a full set of choices or responses to the strategic question. The emphasis will then move to identifying and describing a small number of diverse but feasible choices (i.e., A or B) and the key features of each choice, as well as some pros and cons.

In most cases, the work to frame, analyze, and define choices is conducted by carefully selected working groups with in-depth understanding of both the technical and the business aspects of the strategic question. The individuals chosen need to step out of their normal roles and be able and willing to address the questions from the perspective of the totality of the organization. Each working group is responsible for developing the analysis and choices for a particular set of issues or questions. (In the next section, the roles and structure of the various groups, including working groups, will be considered.) In developing their outputs, the working groups may need to liaise with reference groups and external experts, as well as on a more ad hoc basis with relevant individuals or small groups with particular perspectives. They would also liaise with other working groups to ensure that any linkages (supporting or conflicting) between choices in different topic areas are identified.

3. **Integrated strategic recommendations and priorities.** On selecting the appropriate choice or response for each strategic question, each of the

working groups then finalizes its recommendations and provides supporting rationale. These are presented to the other working groups and also to the strategy integration team (these illustrative roles are described in more detail in the next section), who would then review and consider these responses in an integrated manner. The emphasis, ideally, should be on reaching collective viewpoints, which are then put to the responsible executive leadership team for challenge and ratification. It is possible that the strategy integration team will ask the working groups to provide sufficient evidence and rationale to justify their recommendations and, potentially, to go back and explore more radical choices for analysis and consideration. At this stage in the process, expect considerable dialogue across working groups and intense debate on the most sensitive and far-reaching choices that are being explored.

4. **Integrated strategic plan, directions, and goals.** The first part of this stage focuses on taking the outputs from each working group, that is, the strategic choices recommended, and developing an integrated set of recommendations and decisions for the agency. This should be reasonably high level and include directions and priorities for the agency for the following five or more years.

At this time, working groups would also set out some discrete and hopefully visionary goals for the end of five or more years (or the projected life of the strategic plan), as well as some interim goals or objectives to calibrate the nature and pace of change implied by the recommendations. These objectives should be seen as the binding force for all parts of the organization. All constituents must be able to understand the rationale and implications of the intended strategic direction and be able to take decisions for their area of responsibility to enable the agency to move forward smoothly, doing what needs to be accomplished.

Ideally, once the directions and goals are agreed on (note these may be refinements or updates to previous goals for the agency), they can be articulated in a "strategic results template." (This may already exist as part of the strategic planning and management approach of organizations that already have a consistent planning and performance management framework across their entire international organization.)

This is essentially a tool at an organizational level covering all of the most important objectives, measures, targets, and achievements for all of the main parts of the global organization and that is integrated into the day-to-day management approach. Typically, objectives will be expected to span external and internal items, covering categories such as the following:

1. programmatic approach and impact
2. beneficiaries and local stakeholders
3. donors
4. income
5. internal staff and skills
6. finance management (cost and investment)
7. processes, systems, and infrastructure
8. license to operate

For each area, a small number of specific objectives are defined, with some associated measures and targets over the projected life of the plan. These specific targets can be identified by mapping the strategic goals from the emerging strategic recommendations using subsets of teams selected from various work groups or other functions as required.

Indicative Project Structure

For international development and relief agencies to meet the requirements of a strategic planning process, it is important that they have a clear and transparent project structure for the strategic review. This needs to cover the roles and teams that will manage and deliver the review, as well as the governance and management mechanisms that will guide the process toward an agreed strategic plan. The project structure suggestions that will follow are built on a few important principles, namely, the following.

1. **The need to construct small, carefully selected, and focused working teams for each set of related strategic questions.** Individuals chosen need to have both the knowledge and credibility to address the set of important strategic questions and choices that were prioritized during the early stages of the review and should be able to identify and define meaningful directions and goals that can guide the organization as a whole to achieve its mission.

2. **Achieving the benefit of broad-ranging, thorough, and effective consultation.** This can be critical to the success of a strategic review in this sector. A key element is balancing input from different dimensions of the organization, from the field; from funding offices, affiliates, and central specialist functions; and from external stakeholders.

3. **The need to provide clear structure and transparency so that individuals and groups throughout the organization have the facility to provide useful feedback and input to emerging thinking at a few carefully selected points.** However, it is important that the day-to-day work of the agency—

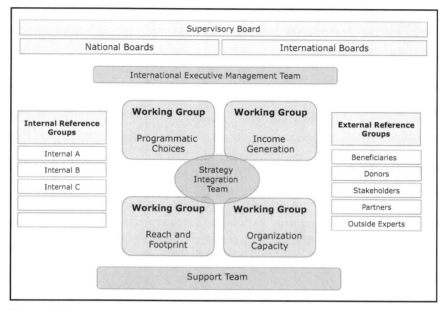

Figure 5.4 Example structure for global strategic review.

delivering programs on the ground—is not unduly distracted by the work of the strategic review. It is also important that the working teams who are analyzing and progressing the questions, choices, and recommendations are not overly distracted by well-meaning but disrupting input or suggestions from individuals throughout the organization. In our experience, this is a considerable risk. Getting the balance right between a desirable level of engagement to ensure stakeholder buy-in and quality input and too much engagement is something that deserves careful consideration at the start of the strategic review.

The "petal diagram" in figure 5.4 provides a visual representation of a possible project structure. It can be seen that there are a number of critical key constituents, which are explained next in terms of role and constituency.

International Boards, Supervisory Board, and National Boards

Large international agencies often have a complex set of boards at the national and international levels. The process of conducting the strategic review therefore needs to be designed to provide the various boards with the visibility and in some cases with direct connection with the progress of the work. Progress across both interim and emerging recommendations should ideally be shared during scheduled reviews.

Alongside this "formal" route, we believe that hands-on participation of a few carefully selected members of the international or supervisory boards can be very beneficial. One option is to nominate a handful of individuals and, for example, ask one representative to join each working team. In this way, the boards can have more intimate contact and provide their own expertise to challenges in appropriate areas. This has the benefit of bringing boards intellectually closer to the evolution of organizational thinking. It can also provide new perspectives and ideas and create a valuable intimacy with the content and the process, which representatives can share with other board members. This ensures a much richer discussion at the board level in the subsequent review and approval process.

In addition to the oversight role of the international boards, it is important that national boards have the opportunity to keep abreast of the process, to give input where it makes sense, and ultimately to be informed and prepared to approve and fully buy into the global strategic plan.

Working Groups

A small number of working groups (normally three to five) can be created to tackle groups of related, prioritized strategic questions. Each group could have approximately four to six members who are selected based on their expertise, experience, and creativity. Importantly, they need to be able to deliberate and make recommendations on behalf of the entire agency, leaving aside the priorities and possibly narrower perspectives of their day-to-day roles. Ensuring that these people are empowered and trusted by the agency is not always easy, but it is an important ingredient for success.

In addition, it may be helpful for each working group to have an **executive sponsor** who will be responsible for creating an effective linkage between the working group and the leadership team. Sponsors should be encouraged to join the dialogue as a peer rather than in their capacity as a member of the executive leadership team. The sponsor should remain sufficiently close to the emerging thinking and analysis to be able to represent emerging thinking and recommendations in deliberations of the international executive leadership team. Working group members will typically be part time, devoting about 25 percent to 50 percent of their time during the intensive Stages 2 and 3 of the review.

Strategy Integration Team

The strategy integration team is the central unit that manages the strategy review process on a day-to-day basis. It works with the international executive leadership team, the working groups, and other key groups to steer the process to its successful conclusion.

For example, at its core, the strategy integration team could have two or three extremely respected and capable full-time people. The composition of the team needs to be designed to (1) have considerable knowledge of the work of the agency, (2) have credibility with senior and middle management, (3) have independent thinkers who are open to new proposals, and (4) be comfortable with the process and decision-making requirements of managing a global strategic review. This team needs to be able to direct, challenge, support, and integrate the thinking of the various working groups. It also needs to be comfortable commissioning the data collection, analysis, or research that members feel is necessary to supplement or test emerging recommendations.

The strategy integration team will work seamlessly with the working group leads, effectively acting as an extended integration team. At the later stages of the review, as the working groups are dissolved, it is possible that some of the working group leads will become part of the strategy integration team helping to draft the final strategic plan.

Strategy Support Team

The strategy support team needs to have the key functional skills to support the strategic review on an ongoing basis. This would usually include three important disciplines:

1. **Internal communications:** This is a significant challenge in a global strategic review. It requires significant input and effort from all who are part of the international executive leadership team and should include carefully designed communications activities.
2. **Business/financial modeling:** A solid set of quantified facts is essential to prompt strategic thinking and test the implications of new strategic directions or recommendations being discussed.

3. **Administration and technical support:** This will ensure that the time of the individuals who contribute to the various groups and meetings, whether through face-to-face or virtual interaction, is used as effectively as possible.

Internal Reference Groups
In contrast to working groups, internal reference groups provide input and feedback based primarily on the perspectives and priorities of their particular part of the agency. Their involvement should be much less onerous than that of working group members, as they input at a few carefully chosen points in the process. For example, they could contribute to the different working groups as the key strategic questions are properly framed and/or later as a sounding board for working group recommendations. Some of these groups may already exist within the agency, while others may be specifically created for the purpose of the review. Typically, members of reference teams will need to devote one to two days per month to fulfill their role.

"Points of Progress": Green, White, and Blue Papers

Given the broad scale and scope of an entire international agency, spanning fifty to one hundred countries and numerous areas of focus, it is important to have clear "points of progress," that is, the milestones to be met by working groups during the strategy process. These milestones will broadly define the extent of the progress made by working groups on a particular strategic question. On reaching these points, it would be important to seek an external reaction from the integration team and from the senior leadership team. These can also be effective points at which to engage reaction and feedback from the reference groups. The following summarizes briefly how this can work:

1. **Green paper:** A short one- to two-page paper for each of the most important strategic questions and issues to be considered, the key discontinuities that currently underlie these questions (opportunity, challenge, problem), and some hypotheses of potential choices with regard to how the organization can respond to these questions. Experience suggests that these papers need to take into consideration the diversity of language and writing

skills across the agency and should therefore be limited to key points only.

2. **White paper:** This is the next iteration of the green paper. It contains a more thorough view of the issues and choices, with firmer data and evidence on the key factors prompting the strategic question. It will have a more developed view of key choices and trade-offs to respond to the strategic question, ideally narrowed down to two to three firm alternatives. These papers could usefully be shared with some or all of the reference teams who could challenge emerging recommendations and provide feedback.

3. **Blue paper—the proposal:** This, the next iteration of the paper, will have a clear recommendation of the preferred choice for the agency, a clear rationale underpinning the choice, and a view of some of the key implications associated with this recommended choice, for example, cost, implied degree of change, and risks.

This process, which needs to be defined by the strategy integration team, should also help to facilitate the input of the reference teams in a timely and effective way and also to allow the strategy integration team and members of the global leadership team to keep abreast of the substance of the review as the work proceeds.

5.5. Example Variations and Permutations

As indicated earlier, there is not just one way of executing a strategic review; neither is there a right or wrong way. In the previous section, we outlined the basic phasing, structure, and mechanics of one possible approach. However, there are a number of variants to that approach, with associated pros and cons.

During the preconsultation phase, a detailed approach needs to be designed to fit within the particular organizational context, as well as with the likely nature of the strategic questions that are expected to be tackled.

Potential variations in the approach will be driven by, for example, the desired pace in conducting the review, especially where there are some large and urgent strategic issues that need to be addressed. Variations can also be influenced by the need for deep participation or the perceived need for a radical overhaul of the agency's strategic direction.

There is sometimes the perception that a highly participative process is likely to produce a less innovative and radical solution. We do not concur with this perspective. If a process is properly constructed and managed, with clear governance and genuine and focused participation, it is possible to identify innovative and radical recommendations. Meaningful participation will also provide a crucial opportunity to help the organization make the necessary transition in thinking and understanding as the strategic review progresses, rather than wait to sell the new ideas when the review is complete. This will make the job of implementing the resultant changes significantly easier. Hence, if the senior leadership team feels that a significant change of course is demanded, participation becomes even more important.

However, if the remit of the strategic review is to provide a confirmation of the mission and direction already in place, merely framing some more specific goals and targets to refine the strategic plan, then a much more focused team structure and simplified review process will suffice. Similarly, if the scope of the strategic questions to be tackled from the outset is very narrow, for example, if there are only one or two big questions that need to be tackled at a fundamental level, then the structure and process need to be adjusted to match.

The following are some possible variations that could be considered. Each of these variants is reviewed in table 5.1, with associated pros and cons, as well as with some suggestions in terms of when such a variant might be suitable.

- **Variation A:** To conduct the review over a longer period of time, something on the order of twelve to eighteen months. This would, potentially, allow for some more logical sequencing of efforts and also allow time for collecting key research data as the work proceeds.
- **Variation B:** To a have a single larger integrated working team, essentially an expanded version of the strategy integration team. In this approach the working groups can still exist but with a much lighter touch, that is, they could help provide input and discuss ideas and choices but would not take full ownership of the work to produce recommendations.
- **Variation C:** Where the international executive leadership team, or a subset of that team, takes on the role of the strategy integration team, ensuring that this team is integrally involved in all aspects of developing the new strategy.

Table 5.1
Some Variations in Approach

Variant	Pros	Cons	Suitable Where
A. Conducting the review over a longer period of time	• Easier to sequence efforts to respond to questions	• Harder to retain engagement within the organization over an extended period (more than six to nine months) • Risk of loss or dilution of momentum in converting emerging directions to clear goals and creating a solid strategic "results template" • Risk of costs of process becoming excessive	• There are one or two crunch questions whose answers are critical to being able to tackle some other questions.
B. A single full-time working group, instead of three to five part-time working groups	• Easier to manage and integrate thinking	• Weaker participation and diversity of expertise devoted to each of the strategic questions	• The scope of strategic questions is narrow. • The organization is able to trust a smaller group of people to consider the key choices and come up with recommendations.
C. The global senior leadership/management team, or subset of, takes on the role of the strategy integration team	• Increases the opportunity of all members of the senior team getting immersed in the thinking and decisions • Increases ownership of the final strategy • Can stimulate some content debate between members of the senior team beyond the normal scope, providing opportunity for a more cohesive team in the long run	• The feasibility of individual team members devoting sufficient time to fulfill this role must be questioned. • Poor interpersonal dynamics between the team can hamper meaningful debate and decision making. • The members of this team may not have a sufficiently open-minded perspective.	• This can be effective where there is a small, well-functioning global leadership team.

5.6. Frequently Asked Questions

Q1: How Long Does a Global Strategic Review Need to Take?

In our experience, excluding the preconsultation phase, the total duration of a strategic review should take between six and nine months.

The preconsultation phase typically takes a minimum of four to six weeks. It can be done over a longer period if preferred. This phase should be understood by the organization as the "shaping and framing" preparatory work for the strategic review, not the actual review.

The central part of the review, that is, Stages 1, 2, and 3, typically take three to six months. In our experience, this is the minimum time needed to be able to create meaningful debate, support that debate with reasonable analysis and the collection of important information, and consider the recommendations in a thoughtful manner. This could be allowed to extend for a longer period; however, this can create a number of risks. First, the organization may not be able to stay focused and may waste undue time getting to concrete recommendations. There is an associated risk that the strategy process may excessively distract the organization from its day-to-day work. In addition, the best people whom you want at the center of the thought process may become increasingly interrupted by unavoidable calls on their time from day-to-day issues.

The final phase, namely, producing an integrated strategic plan, typically takes one to two months. Again, this should not be dragged out, as it will risk loss of focus and undermine the momentum created during the core stages of the review.

Q2: How Much Should the International Board and the Various Other Boards Be Engaged During the Strategic Review?

It is important to engage the various boards in a clear and genuine manner, both in advance of a strategic review and during the preconsultation phase. They need to be consulted on the timing and scope of the review and be aware of how they will be kept informed and, in some cases, can contribute to the progress of the review. They also need to be aware and very clearly understand at what points in the strategic review processes they will be called on to make decisions.

During the core stages of the work, having a small number of carefully selected board members involved in a hands-on capacity can be very valuable. They could, for example, contribute as ordinary work group members based on their particular experience and expertise. However, it is important that their participation at this level is as an ordinary working group member and that their board-level status does not give their opinions and contributions any more weight than those of other work group members.

Q3: What Is an Example of a Key Strategic Question?

This will be different in every situation. Some that we have come across include the following:

1. Should our agency fully adopt a rights-based approach in how it does its programming? If so, what would that mean on the ground, and how does it impact our long-term funding strategy?
2. Today, the poor and disadvantaged on the planet are spread across poor, middle-income, and rich countries. Should we abandon the distinction in our model between (1) funding countries and (2) program countries, and should we run programs in the North and in the South?
3. Should we focus exclusively on one area of development need or domain, which gives us greater focus and differentiation, or should we engage with all development domains?
4. What is the core competence of the agency? How does this need to evolve and be strengthened for the future?

Q4: Should You Consult With Stakeholders in Poor Communities, That Is, the Beneficiaries?

Proper and genuine consultation at the appropriate times and levels can be very useful but needs to be very carefully carried out to be practical and meaningful. Too often, consultation at this level is symbolic, not representative, or the input is not available in time to be useful. In the future, when agencies have more robust planning, performance, and accountability processes, with ongoing and systematic feedback from all stakeholders, this kind of information can be considered on a continuous basis.

Q5: How Do You Deal With the Logistics of Enabling Teams to Contribute Effectively and Work as High-Performing Units When They Are Scattered Across the World?

While the detailed mechanics of the day-to-day work of the working groups will differ according to the agency in question, achieving timely progress is likely to involve a reasonable amount of face-to-face interaction, in addition to ongoing virtual work. Typically, working groups will need at least two to three concentrated face-to-face working sessions over several days (usually a full week) during the intensive analysis and planning period.

However, considerable progress can be made by effective delegation of responsibilities and tasks within the working groups, as well as by making effective use of technology for review of analysis and sharing of information. In fact, we have found that some agencies have discovered the real benefits of an effective virtual team working through the work of a strategic review and have subsequently carried forward this possibility to many ongoing program and management activities. Increasingly, there are some very useful online collaboration tools that can make remote working easier.

Q6: Who Decides, and How Do Decisions Get Made in Practice?

There is a formal and informal answer to this question. Earlier, at a working group level, decisions should ideally emerge through consensus from the group. This typically (though not always) occurs as groups debate the necessary facts or information and reach a shared understanding of the key aspects related to a particular issue. In certain cases, a working group may seek guidance from the global leadership team on a particular issue.

Formally, the global leadership team will decide on the key strategic recommendations that go to the international and other boards for review and agreement. It would, however, be unusual for this team to make a decision that was not in line with the views of a working group that it had entrusted to tackle the issue. Indeed, as individual members of the global team may also sit as normal members of working groups, or as "executive sponsors," debate should ideally be going on at both levels on some of the most important issues during the intensive periods of the review.

It should be borne in mind that one of the key definitions of success for a strategic review is to bring the organization together intellectually and emotionally and to create alignment behind the future direction of the organization.

Q7: How Do You Achieve a Balance Between Gaining Clarity in Terms of Direction and Goals and Retaining the Flexibility to Respond to Ongoing Changes in the External Environment?

The strategic recommendations and resulting goals set at the latter stages of the strategic review, plus the strategic results template referred to in section 5.4, provide a clear set of targets to guide the implementation of the strategic plan. However, it is important to realize that a strategic plan is not a rigid "straitjacket" for the organization. Senior management needs to be able to respond to major unanticipated external events when they emerge. However, this needs to be the exception rather than the norm.

The existence of a clear strategic plan is a vital step in being able to change course should the need arise and is particularly useful in being able to explain any change in course with stakeholders inside and outside the organization. **Put bluntly, it is very hard to explain a change in course unless you are very clear on the direction you are already traveling in.** Without that clarity, new demands tend to be added to an already overloaded, poorly prioritized agenda, and the ultimate effectiveness of the contribution of the agency is likely to be severely diminished. This is historically an area where INGOs have had challenges and is something that can be addressed by using the strategic plan as a tool to align planning, budgeting, and one-off projects and initiatives.

Q8: How Do You Ensure That an Organization Is Energized During the Review and During the Implementation of the New Strategic Plan?

This is a very important issue to consider as you plan the design of the process of a strategic review. In addition, you need to reflect carefully on the balance of the emerging recommendations. One way of doing this is to ensure a reasonable balance between what we call the **motivating glue** for the agency, which is the glue that inspires people to be part of the agency's mission, and what we call the **enabling glue**, which is those necessary, enabling processes and systems that form the functional backbone of an international agency and that are often a considerable challenge to progress.

A big mistake is to derive a set of recommendations that lean too much, or exclusively, on the enabling glue rather than the motivating glue of the agency. Excessive emphasis on enabling may well be a rational response to some of the major strategic questions; however, it is important that an agency also builds on and strengthens its motivating glue, positioning changes and efforts to strengthen enabling systems, processes, and structures in terms of their contribution to the motivating glue of the organization. A step we strongly recommend in the preconsultation stage is conducting working sessions to understand the motivating glue that binds the organization together and that is important to attract and retain key staff in the organization.

Q9: How Do You Ensure That the Strategic Plan Gets Implemented?

Translating the results of a strategic review into an implementable plan is a key challenge. It is all too easy for working groups to get disbanded as the recommendations are agreed on and move back to their normal roles before a very clear set of strategic goals is clearly defined. There are a few important steps that we would recommend.

1. Clear tangible goals need to be defined for each of the strategic recommendations before key people from the work groups are released back into their normal roles. There is nothing more frustrating or wasteful than having new people who do not have the depth of understanding of what was intended trying to create goals and plans after the strategic review is completed.

2. These tangible goals need to be mapped (by the same people) onto a strategic results template. This is essentially a balanced scorecard showing how the changes demanded are mapped onto various components of the organization, for example, policy and methodology, roles and skills, processes and systems, culture and behavior, fund-raising, cost and investment, infrastructure and structure. Where there is a preexisting and well-functioning global planning and performance framework with performance areas and associated processes, this step will be significantly easier.

3. The results template needs to encompass different constituents of the organization, for example, program offices, funding offices, and central or shared functions, and each will then need to do its own local business planning as part of its own planning cycle.

4. Ideally, a strategy implementation lead with a deep understanding of the strategy and strong credibility throughout the organization should be appointed to oversee the changes implied by the new strategic plan, be they new initiatives or changes that get embedded into organizational or business plans for different units of the organization.

5. The investment in financial and management time needs to be clearly specified before the plan is finalized. If there are insufficient resources or "organizational bandwidth" to follow through on what is recommended, it is far better to adjust the timing or phasing and, if necessary, to prioritize. This is better than losing credibility later when the expectations of those who contributed to the plan, as well as the organization at large, are not met.

6. The pace of the implementation needs to be sufficiently rapid so that the organization sees the concrete impacts of the new strategic plan early and the positive momentum created by the planning process itself is maintained. As a guideline, we recommend that the "half-life" of the implementation is completed on the order of twelve to eighteen months. By that we mean that at least half of all of the changes implied by the new strategic plan are in place within eighteen months.

Notes

1. Robert S. Kaplan and David P. Norton, *The Balanced Scorecard* (Boston, MA: Harvard Business School Press, 1996).

2. Paul R. Niven, *Balanced Scorecard for Government and Nonprofit Agencies* (Hoboken, NJ: John Wiley, 2008).

3. Paul Ronalds, *The Change Imperative: Creating the Next Generation NGO* (Sterling, VA: Kumarian Press, 2010).

6

Strategic Goals

Integrated Planning & Accountability framework

Stakeholders

Partners

Beneficiaries

Business and financial planning

Individual performance management

Integrated Planning and Accountability for International NGOs

Abstract

This chapter is intended for senior leaders and board members of international NGOs (INGOs) who are concerned about creating a high-performing INGO, facilitated by a robust integrated planning and accountability approach. *Accountability* is a much used and discussed term, particularly to external stakeholders in the development sector, be it donors, beneficiaries, local stakeholders, or other civil society partners. However, the central message of this chapter is that external accountability has little credibility unless it is an integral part of an effective and integrated planning and accountability process. Integrated planning and accountability are part of the lifeblood of any high-performing international organization.

An integrated planning and accountability framework is likely to have four main components. First, it should include a set of consistent "performance scorecards" for all parts of the agency, encompassing objectives, metrics, and targets. Second, it should have clear processes for target setting and monitoring that are integral parts of the day-to-day management process and connect with strategic goals, business and financial planning, and individual performance management. Third, it should have clearly defined roles, indicating who is involved in facilitating, challenging, or approving target setting and monitoring. Finally, it should have a set of guidelines around the behaviors that are encouraged through the planning and accountability process.

Efforts to strengthen the accountability framework require careful consideration of a number of important and interconnected components of an organization's make-up, such as strategic goals, leadership behaviors, and organization structure. It also needs to work in tandem with important enabling processes such as finance, human resource management, and information management. This chapter explores these dimensions and reviews some of the typical challenges and blockages that may exist for some INGOs. It provides ideas and insights to address these, but we fully recognize that progress will require effort and rigor. Crucially, it may also require a considerable change in management style, discipline, and behavior.

A range of newer initiatives such as the International NGO Accountability Charter and the Global Reporting Initiative are extremely useful in drawing attention to external accountability as an important ingredient for the legitimacy and success of any international agency. However, the act of producing an annual accountability report that is separate from the real process of day-to-day management is, though useful, not sufficient.

6.1. The Concept of Accountability

This is the first part of a two-part introduction. First, it is useful to reflect on the concept of "accountability." What exactly is meant by accountability for INGOs? To whom are INGOs accountable? And for what? As we review the literature, we soon realize that this is a complex topic.

The second section introduces the case for integrated planning and accountability as an "inside-out" view from within large INGOs. Here we will explore some frequently observed challenges and opportunities and investigate what role integrated planning and accountability can play in responding to these issues.

The Concept of Accountability

The concept of accountability is often associated with the idea of "holding someone to account." If I purchase a new iPhone in an Apple store, as a customer, I expect the product to do what is said on the box. If there is a fault, I can hold Apple to account. This accountability to me is reinforced formally by consumer law but also informally by Apple's interest in protecting its reputation and brand. Furthermore, if Apple damages the environment in the manufacturing process, it may well be held to account by governments, society at large through pressure groups, and of course by customers who may look less favorably on its products in the future.

When an individual stands for high political office, the candidate usually declares what he or she stands for and intends to do. If voters support this promise, they then have the opportunity to hold him or her to account at the time of the next election. This is a voluntary agreement between both parties. Citizens can be held to account to comply with laws of the state where they are resident. In this case, this is not a voluntary agreement, as the individual may not have the opportunity to live elsewhere.

To whom are companies in the private sector accountable? In the past, the notion of "accountability to shareholders" would feature very prominently in a typical response, that is, to the main financial investors in the company. However, over the past few decades the water has been muddied. It is pretty much accepted that this response is simplistic and not sufficient. Many companies now talk about the triple bottom line. In addition to financial results, they often speak about a bottom line in terms of social good, as well as of the impact on the environment. The concept of accountability to a broader set of stakeholders is becoming more of an intrinsic part of how businesses think and act. A practical manifestation of this is the evolution of corporate social responsibility (CSR) in many private businesses. This is explored in some detail in a major research study, *Connecting Business and Development*, released in 2009,[1] and also in the recent *Business in Development Study 2012*, released in September 2012.[2]

So what are we to conclude? Accountability to whom and for what is not a clear-cut idea, even for private businesses. Shareholders have the right to withdraw their support from specific enterprises and close them down if they so desire. But so can society at large, customers, and employees who prefer to use their time and skills elsewhere. In addition, accountability can be in the form of formal and informal agreements and may or may not be voluntary.

Accountability of International NGOs

So what does accountability mean for large INGOs? When we reflect on the origins of INGOs, we see most started on a fully voluntary basis where committed individuals came together, choosing to contribute their time, energy, and resources to a particular cause they felt passionate about, such as a famine, poverty or injustice, or the effects of war. They were motivated by a spirit of giving and sharing and in certain cases were following through on a postcolonial sense of responsibility. And of course some were inspired by religious convictions. Over the past fifty years, many INGOs have grown into very large, complex organizations that have transformed in their scope and scale and also in the rigor and professionalism of their programs. However, irrespective of their origins, the question of accountability has always been an area of sensitivity for these organizations.

So who are INGOs accountable to? And for what? We can expect that NGOs are accountable to a range of external stakeholders in the development process: to beneficiaries, to local institutions, to civil society partners, and of course to the donors who provide the funding. However, when we explore a little deeper into each of these groups, we find that what accountability means is not so straightforward.

First, let's reflect on the large donors who provide large grants to fund many development and humanitarian programs. Clearly, donors have some right to monitor the progress and impact of the work they support. They can reasonably expect to hold the NGO to account and have the right to withdraw their financial support if the NGO does not deliver the outputs or contribution that they expect. However, what if donors do not understand what good development requires and are biased toward interventions that are contrary to good development practice? Do NGOs just do as they are told? And to what extent do they have a responsibility to reeducate donors on which interventions are most useful in different situations?

INGOs clearly need to be accountable to local beneficiaries and other important stakeholders, in particular, local communities, local community-based organizations, and other local civil society organizations. However, it would be simplistic to assume that all of these constituents had a consistent set of views and priorities. How should an NGO balance these conflicting perspectives? And of course where local abuse of power and rights by a local set of stakeholders may be a contributory blockage to progress, how then can we deal with accountability for these particular stakeholders?

Finally, governments at a local or national level are also important stakeholders in social and economic progress, be they elected or otherwise. What if these governments distrust or dislike the help that is being offered by INGOs or are minded to manipulate programs that NGOs are there to support?

Clearly, defining accountability is not so simple.

So What Are We to Do?

The purpose of this chapter is not intended to answer this set of very important, thorny, and perhaps sometimes what seem like philosophical questions. However, there is a need to acknowledge that these questions exist and that INGOs need to find a way through.

We would like to make a few important points that provide a useful context for the rest of this chapter. First, there is a need to recognize there are a wide variety of external stakeholders, and their views and feedback need to be meaningfully represented in the planning and accountability processes of any large INGO. This is akin to customer input and feedback mechanisms for any commercial firm. Over time, an agency will get more adept at collecting this information in a systematic manner and also improve its capacity to use this input in its planning and decision-making processes.

Second, there is a growing recognition of the need to rebalance the amount of attention devoted to different external stakeholders. In particular, it is accepted that beneficiaries and local community organizations need to have a more meaningful voice in terms of what is planned in future programs, as well as provide useful and honest feedback on the success of completed programs. There is much discourse to this effect but not enough in terms of practical progress.

Third, we recognize that strategic initiatives such as the International NGO Accountability Charter[3] are a major step forward in drawing attention to external accountability as an important ingredient in the planning and management processes of an INGO. However, the act, for example, of producing an annual accountability report that is separate from the real process of day-to-day planning and management is of limited value. This risks being little more than a public relations exercise, akin to CSR reporting in the early days of corporate dabbling in social responsibility.

However, the central point is this. **External accountability without strong internal accountability has little credibility. Without a robust and joined-up planning and performance management process that brings together the contributions of all parts of an international agency, any discussion about external accountability to partners, stakeholders, and beneficiaries is just hollow talk.**

This chapter is intended to help with this challenge. We believe this is an area of considerable weakness for many INGOs and is an essential foundation stone to be able to get "off the back foot" in the debate about accountability, legitimacy, and impact.

6.2. The Call From Within: For Clarity and Alignment

Approximately eight years ago, in one of my very early assignments in this sector, we were tasked with reviewing the management and leadership practices of a very large INGO. This was a successful, established, and growing organization and had within its sights the ambition of becoming a US$1 billion agency.

As part of the investigation, we had the privilege to spend time in field programs across the world, in five of the poorest countries in Africa, and with program staff from Asia and Central and South America. We met individually with the vast majority of the country and regional directors in the field and ran informal sessions with some of their staff. In addition, we also held discussions with the senior teams of a number of the large income generating offices in the North. This was truly a baptism of fire to the world of international development and INGOs.

During the course of this investigation, there were many aspects that were truly impressive. It was easy to be bowled over by the enthusiasm and Trojan efforts of the staff in the field, their commitment, their facilitation skills, and their ingenuity in the most trying of circumstances. We were impressed by the quality of many of the development professionals we interacted with. Many were highly qualified with master's and doctorate degrees in development and associated topics, as well as with many years of practical experience in the field. They were clearly dedicating their entire careers to improving the lives of those in need of help, constantly striving to achieve ever more scalable and lasting impacts. Moreover, we were captivated by the joy, smiles, and hope in all those gorgeous African faces in the local communities in poor rural areas and in urban slums in sub-Sahara Africa that the efforts that such NGOs seemed to ignite.

Frequently Observed Issues

However, as we listened and probed across the various constituents of this organization, mixed into much of the positive impressions, there were a number of strong and concerning issues. We now know that these challenges were not unique to that particular agency; in fact they have reappeared again and again in the course of the assignments that Morgana and I have had the privilege of participating in over the past eight years. What are these challenges?

One can often get the sense of a somewhat low-risk environment, where many very talented staff and managers seem to have noticeable fear of stepping outside accepted norms. There is often a considerable frustration with the difficulty of capturing, sharing, and using knowledge and learning across the entire organization, to avoid reinventing the wheel, to build on what had been achieved and learned elsewhere, and to avoid approaches that have already proved to be unsuccessful.

In many agencies, one has to work hard to appreciate the natural tensions that seem to prevail between the major constituents of the global organization, most notably between the field offices, the regional offices, the center or headquarters, and the income-generation offices in the North. The latter frequently have independent boards and in a number of cases can appear as reluctant participants in their particular global organizational construct.

Too often, there is an impression of a degradation of positive energy and organizational atmosphere as one moves up through the hierarchy of an agency, from field to country office, from country office to regional office, and from regional office to headquarters. Sometimes, one gets the impression that different constituents of the organization are not meaningfully aligned in terms of their goals and priorities. The expectation of synergy and cohesion is sometimes not what one might expect.

And when one tries to understand and dissect the management style and approach, in some cases one can see evidence of what could be characterized as a "personality-based" culture, often associated with a bias toward a command and control style of management, which we referred to in chapter 1 as a "relational" style of management.

In this early assignment, it became clear that one of the important blockages contributing to many of these challenges was staring us in the face. When we listened carefully to managers and staff across the organization, we heard an overwhelming and vociferous call for a clearer definition of "good performance" and a stronger and consistent focus on performance management at an organizational level. Put simply, it was a desire for a consistent, transparent, and enduring definition of goals, objectives, and targets, not just for their particular area but also for all parts of the organization. Many of the managers and staff were openly frustrated by the continued tolerance for underachievement, for poor performance, and for poor performers.

It became obvious that the definition of good performance was either too limited, not transparent, or varied depending on who was in charge. When a new country director was appointed, the country team had to learn to decipher his or her management philosophy and to relearn what "good" looked like. To complicate matters further, when each new senior executive arrived from a regional office, from the center, or from one of the powerful income-generating offices, he or she invariably had additional advice, guidance, or priorities to heap on top of an already overloaded workload.

Program staff in the field were clearly struggling with overload and with misaligned and sometimes conflicting priorities. They were vociferous in their desire for transparency, consistency, and continuity. They wanted to have clarity on the goals, measures, and targets so that they, and others, could plan and track their progress and performance. They also wanted other parts of the organization to have similar clarity and transparency with a consistent approach so that they could know what to expect from others and hence be able to work better as a "synergistic" international team.

As for many INGOs, one can get the impression that the structures and the lines of reporting seem reasonably clear. However, the planning and management processes frequently do not function properly and are not fit for purpose. In our work with a broad range of INGOs, we have been taken aback, again and again, by how this is a critical area of weakness for almost every organization.

Perceived Barriers to Progress

However, when we introduce the idea of an integrated, transparent approach to planning and accountability with very senior-level executives at international levels, we often receive mixed reactions and in some cases open resistance. Many readily recognize that this is something that needs to be done. Some are beginning to make useful progress. Some are daunted by the organizational and governance constructs that make implementation more problematic than it might be in other sectors. Some are deflected by the view that it is not possible to measure outputs and outcomes in a way that is meaningful across the entirety of what the agency does. Others point to the particular characteristic of this sector where those who pay are often different and far away from those who ultimately benefit, highlighting the need for an effective feedback loop. (Arguably, this is not that different for the public sector in areas such as health and education.) Some point to a culture of autonomy, specificity of context, and difficulty of information provision. And some are mindful of the memory of previous unsuccessful attempts to make useful progress.

This journey is not an easy one, but it is one that has been tackled to a very useful degree in both the private sector and public sector over recent decades. Let us briefly reflect on the journey and experiences in the private sector.

Integrated Planning and Accountability in the Private Sector

The concept of integrated planning, performance management, and accountability in large global organizations is relatively young, even in the private sector. BP achieved considerable public and academic praise for its leadership in this area in the 1990s with the philosophy and ideas called "planning and performance management," which were highly credited for BP's impressive and sustained growth and success over this period.[4] The concept of a "balanced scorecard" as a widely applied idea only became popular over the same period, helped by the very useful research and ideas from Kaplan and Norton,[5] first published in the *Harvard Business Review* in 1992.[6]

As for the development and humanitarian sectors, there was often a considerable degree of resistance in the private sector to making substantive progress to efforts to put in place integrated planning and accountability frameworks. In 2002, as part of an assignment to help a large international private sector organization implement a unified planning and performance framework, we came across many of the same barriers.

In this particular assignment, we categorized those who were most resistant to change into three camps. The first camp were managers of divisions and departments who felt they were already performing at a high level and that this was a waste of time and would result only in additional futile intervention by more senior administrators from headquarters who did not understand or appreciate the nuances of their own division. The second camp included those who knew all too well that their performance was below expectations and would prefer not to have additional light cast on their challenges. And the final camp, those in the middle, might prefer to "meander" on rather than discover that more might be expected of them. And of course for the CEO and some other top senior executives, there was sometimes a concern that such a transparent, consistent, and enduring approach would stand in the way of their flexibility to nudge the organization this way or that from their privileged position at the helm. Hence, irrespective of where you looked, there were points of resistance.

As part of this assignment, we conducted a study tour of some leading international private sector organizations across a variety of industry sectors that we felt demonstrated good practice around this topic. Our investigations led to a number of important lessons:

1. The planning and performance management system was the lifeblood of large international organizations that wanted a meaningful connection (two-way) between the strategy and execution of an organization.
2. The existence of such a framework is an enabler to innovation and creativity, not a barrier. Once management and staff have a shared understanding of the goals and targets, they can devote all their energy to meet and exceed these targets.
3. The level of detail needs to be kept at a manageable level, ideally at the level of one, two, or three pages, not large reports. These summaries should draw from existing information that is ideally readily available and not require significant additional data gathering.
4. The process and disciplines around the framework are as important as the actual goals and targets that are put in place.
5. The nature of the approach and framework needs to be adapted to reflect the nature of the industry.

Suffice it to say that this large international company managed to overcome early resistance, and this new approach quickly became second nature to the day-to-day management of that particular organization.

Looking more broadly, since the 1980s there has been major progress in designing and implementing integrated planning and accountability process for many large private sector organizations. This has been stimulated by the growing pressures on large global businesses, which need to be responsive to local contexts on the one hand and on the other hand take advantage of the economies of scope and scale that their stakeholders expect.

Closer to home, when working at Accenture, I remember specifically the first arrival of the first version of a consistent planning and management framework, where the transition had many of the same characteristics. This was a major step forward in making us a more aligned and high-performing global organization. While our approach has gone through many iterations and refinements over the years, it would be inconceivable today to be a high-performance global organization without such a framework.

Case for Change in the Development Sector

After we worked on a variety of assignments in the development and humanitarian sector, it became clear that the progress established in the private (and public) sector had much relevance for international development and humanitarian agencies. As we concluded in chapter 1, the planning, performance management, and accountability processes for INGOs are often too weak and narrow, subjective, or just not helpful enough. In addition, the traditional "relational" style of management, which is characterized by big personalities, strong historic personal relationships, line of sight supervision, and in certain cases a command and control bias, is no longer appropriate for modern, professional, and large-scale INGOs.

A professional and rigorous approach will be a critical facilitator in becoming a joined-up, aligned agency. It can help ensure that objectives and success criteria are transparent and that the contribution of every part of the global organization is explicit and aligned with the organizational goals. It can also help ensure that the voices of key partners and beneficiaries are heard and integrated into the ongoing planning and decision making. All this will support the aim of maximizing the performance and contribution of everything the agency does.

This does not imply complex systems or reams of reports. It does imply the need for alignment on some very carefully selected pieces of performance information, including metrics around areas such as program quality and impact, people, money, and stakeholder satisfaction. An essential part of this requirement is the need for discipline and a management process, creating a forward-looking, constructive management and learning environment.

We fully appreciate that this journey is not an easy one and that it will take time and patience to achieve the right approach for this sector and for each individual agency. There will be particular challenges, for example, from the fragmented governance structures, the established leadership culture and habits, and the unique nature of the work in this sector. However, we believe that it is a journey that is both fully achievable and absolutely essential.

6.3. Understanding Integrated Planning and Accountability

The need for an integrated planning and accountability framework is as important for large development and relief agencies as it is for any large commercial organization. It is the nerve center through which executives, managers, and staff throughout the organization align their efforts and priorities, making adjustments over time as new information and learning is uncovered. Without it, the overall performance of the agency will be significantly less than it could be.

The analogy of the human body is a powerful way of bringing this to life, as described in the following box. This shows how the skeleton, muscles, and brain can be seen as analogous to the structure, capacity, and leadership processes, respectively. The planning and accountability framework is akin to the nervous system, enabling messages to be sent around the body and facilitating the various parts of the body to work together in a coherent manner.

Human Body Analogy

The analogy of the human body is a powerful way to bring to life the need for an integrated planning and accountability framework. The skeleton is an essential part of the human body, as it enables us to keep upright and provides the frame or structure to enable our agility and movement. This is akin to the structure of a large international organization. The muscles and ligaments give power, working with the skeleton to enable us to walk, run, lift, and do physical work. This is similar to the skills, processes, systems, strength, and capacity of an organization to achieve results. The brain is the processor of information, makes major decisions, and sends instructions. This is analogous to the strategy and leadership throughout an organization.

The planning and accountability framework is similar to the nervous system: it enables messages to be sent to and from the brain, and it facilitates the brain, the skeleton, and the muscles to communicate and work together to do what needs to be done. Without the nervous system, the other parts of the body are effectively paralyzed. If it is not functioning properly or works slowly or incorrectly, the performance of the body is diminished. Similarly, for any large international organization, without an effective planning and accountability system, the overall performance of the agency will be significantly less than it could be.

What Are the Important Characteristics?

What are the most important characteristics of a planning and accountability framework? At its simplest level, an integrated planning and accountability framework provides the glue to join the dots between strategic goals, business and financial planning, and individual plans and performance across the organization. This is illustrated in figure 6.1.

When we explore at a deeper level, we can see that that it can play a number of important roles.

Figure 6.1 Joining the dots: Integrated planning and accountability.

1. A Central "Cog" in an Integrated Organizational System

When we look more broadly, we see that integrated performance and accountability are essential enabling and binding cogs in a broader organizational system. This central role is illustrated in figure 6.2. It facilitates a number of important dimensions of the organization to work in harmony, being tailored, for example, to reflect the strategic goals, organizational structure, and leadership style of the agency. It needs to connect smoothly with some of the essential enabling processes of the organization, such as business and financial planning, individual performance planning and management, and other human resource development areas. It also needs to be aligned with the important information and data management processes. Why is this important? Put simply, if strategy, leadership style, performance management, budgeting, planning, and HR processes contradict each other, staff and management will be distracted by unnecessary misalignment and confusion.

2. Connects Global Strategic Goals to Function, Sector, and Geography Goals

An effective, integrated planning and accountability framework acts as an essential glue to translate the overall strategic goals and objectives into the goals and expectations throughout the organization. Overall objectives and targets for the totality of the organization should work in tandem with **local plans**

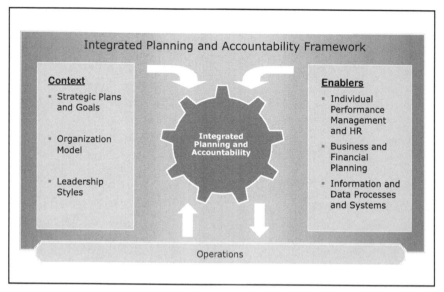

Figure 6.2 Integrated planning and accountability as part of an integrated organizational system.

at regional, country, sector, or functional levels. This is further illustrated in figure 6.3 on the left side of the diagram.

In a matrix structure where the idea of "dual citizenship" is embraced, it is important that the planning process takes time to align goals and metrics from, say, the geographical lines of responsibility (country and regions) with other dimensions of the matrix such as lines of business and expertise.

All of these plans should align directly with the financial planning and budgeting cycles. This alignment is often a challenge and requires considerable tenacity because of the complex legal and governance structures that sometimes exist and also the practical challenges, for example, when different parts of the organization do not have a common financial year.

3. Connects Individual Performance Goals to Organizational Goals

These specific organizational goals, metrics, and targets are important parts of the integrated framework and are a key anchor to define what is required at an individual level. Hence, they should inform the process to plan individual performance agreements. The process of individual performance planning and management can be a powerful mechanism to align individual efforts with the strategic goals and priorities of the agency.

There will be other important inputs at an individual level; for example, the desired leadership behaviors and styles are also a major component. That is, the "how" managers go about their work is often regarded as equally important as the "what" they are seeking to achieve in terms of tangible results. This is illustrated in figure 6.3 on the right side of the diagram.

4. Creates a Robust Mechanism to Connect the Board With the Direction and Performance of an Organization
At the pinnacle of the planning and accountability framework will be a summary set of the most important performance metrics and targets, which can allow the board to have a clear, meaningful, and enduring lens on the direction and progress of the agency. This should provide a meaningful way for the board to hold the CEO and senior leadership to account. Assuming sufficient transparency, this should also help drive alignment throughout the organization, from the boardroom to the work in the field.

5. An Essential Mechanism to Help Implement a New Strategic Plan
A strong integrated planning and accountability framework provides a ready mechanism to translate the directions and priorities created in a new strategic plan into the goals and metrics across the entire organization.

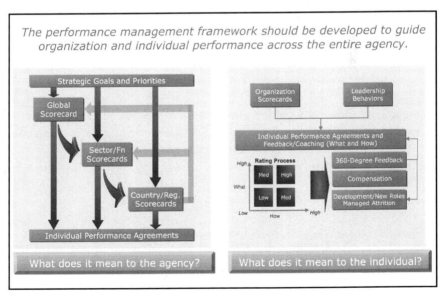

Figure 6.3 Link to individual performance management.

It is worth pausing to consider how a strategic plan fits into the day-to-day planning and management process of an INGO. Unfortunately, as discussed in the previous chapter, strategic reviews can frequently be accused of becoming an island of analysis, debate, and decisions and not being sufficiently connected to the previous progress, direction, and future goals and momentum of an organization.

6.4. What a Framework Might Look Like in This Sector

Moving from the general characteristics to practical specifics, we ask what would an integrated planning and performance framework look like for a large INGO?

Four Primary Components

At a basic level, there are four primary components:

1. a set of consistent, cascading, **balanced scorecards** for all parts of the agency;
2. clear **processes** for target setting and monitoring that are integral parts of the day-to-day planning and management process;
3. clearly defined **roles** indicating who is involved in facilitating, challenging, or approving target setting and monitoring; and
4. a set of guidelines around the **behaviors** that are expected to be encouraged through the planning and accountability process.

Before expanding on each of these components, we fully acknowledge that many INGOs will already have many parts of this framework already in place, at least to some degree. Some are currently working on initiatives to strengthen and develop their planning and accountability processes. Hence, we are suggesting not that this is necessarily new but merely that it is an area that may need to be strengthened so that international agencies can be more confident of delivering a contribution that is more than the sum of the parts. Next, we will expand briefly on each of these four components.

1. A Set of Consistent, Cascading Performance Scorecards

First, at the heart of the framework is a set of scorecards for each of the major constituents of the organization, at country, regional, and global levels, that have a consistent structure and set of definitions; bring together the overall objectives, metrics, and targets; and form an important foundation for the day-to-day planning and management process across the entire organization.

At the top of the organization, the overall agency scorecard, which is part of the same consistent framework, should represent the collective accountability of the global leadership team. This will also provide a lens for the board to be able to understand and monitor the progress of the overall organization and a clear and focused way to hold the CEO and the senior leadership team to account.

Each scorecard would embrace a consistent set of areas of accountability that are carefully selected and designed to encompass aspects such as program quality, staff, income, costs, as well as feedback from key external stakeholders. Bringing all of these areas together is a very important part of the benefits, allowing management to achieve a better balance between different sets of interests; for example, one frequently hears the need to achieve a better balance between the power and the influence of large donors, and the views of beneficiaries and other local stakeholders. An illustrative outline of one such indicative scorecard is shown in figure 6.4.

Each scorecard would cover the most important objectives, metrics, and targets for that part of the organization and form part of a joined-up hierarchy

Performance Area	Value Levers	Objectives	Metric	Score Last Time	Target Score	Trend
Program Quality and Impact	➢ Approach ➢ Outputs ➢ Impact					
Beneficiary/Local Stakeholders	➢ Planning ➢ Participation ➢ Satisfaction					
Donors	➢ Strategic relationships ➢ Satisfaction					
Income	➢ Growth ➢ Mix ➢ Cost					
Internal Staff and Skills	➢ Satisfaction ➢ Skills ➢ Behaviors					
Finance Management	➢ Overhead ➢ Efficiency ➢ ROI					
Processes and Systems	➢ Compliance ➢ Satisfaction ➢ Learning					
License to Operate	➢ Compliance ➢ Reputation/Brand					

Guide of ten to twenty carefully selected metrics in total, for each node of the organization.

Figure 6.4 Outline of balanced scorecard (illustrative).

Performance Area	National/ Fund- raising Offices	Country Offices/ Field Programs	Regions	Lines of Business and Expertise	Global Scorecard
Program Quality and Impact					
Beneficiary/Local Stakeholders					
Donors					
Income					
Internal Staff and Skills					
Finance Management					
Processes and Systems					
License to Operate					

Figure 6.5 Consistent scorecard framework for all nodes of the organization.

that gives clarity and transparency to the expected contributions of all parts of the organization (see figure 6.5).

Ideally, when designing the scorecard structure, an organization would strive for what are often described as "balanced" scorecards. Balanced typically means two things. First, there should be a balance between the different factors or areas that contribute to the overall goals of the organizations, including aspects such as program quality, staff skills and well-being, enabling systems, and external stakeholder feedback. Second, there should be a balance between "leading" indicators and "lagging" indicators. Leading indicators are forward-looking metrics and give a signal as to how an organization is likely to perform or contribute in the future, where the full results of current efforts are some way off. Lagging indicators help an organization understand the outcomes and impact of past decisions and efforts.

2. Processes and Disciplines
Second, there should be clear processes for target setting and monitoring that are integral parts of the day-to-day management process. This should describe the frequency of reporting (e.g., monthly or quarterly) and also specify any recommended peer reviews. These can be very useful to create horizontal chal-

lenge and to help alignment across different organizational units. These processes should link directly with business and financial planning processes and also with the individual performance management process.

In addition, there should be a clear understanding by management at the different levels of the organization as to how the information will be used to support key decision making on a day-to-day basis. This is an important part of integrated planning and accountability.

3. Roles

There should be clearly defined roles indicating who is to be involved in facilitating, challenging, or approving targets and also who is involved in monitoring progress against targets.

It is particularly important that individuals who have strong credibility within the organization own the task of facilitating the planning and accountability process, as well as compiling the performance information.

4. Guidelines and Desired Behaviors

Finally, there should be a set of guidelines around the behaviors that are expected to be encouraged through the planning of an accountability process, when the new framework becomes part of the normal discipline of day-to-day management. A good example of a desired behavior is that the performance reviews should be forward looking and constructive, taking a coaching approach to help deliver best future outcomes, avoiding a temptation to devote excessive attention to detailed micro analysis of reasons for past underperformance. Ideally, the balance here should be 80 percent forward looking and 20 percent reflecting on the outcomes of past decisions.

At the planning stage, when metrics and targets are being designed and agreed on, it is also important to encourage an appropriate degree of stretch so that targets are stretching though meaningful. Care also needs to be taken to ensure that targets are reasonably aligned and consistent with what others are seeking to achieve in other parts of the organization.

Principles or Guidelines Based on Past Experience

The following are some guidelines based on some practical experience in the private sector on equivalent initiatives:

- Integrated planning and accountability is **not a straitjacket.** It is a framework that can be leaned on to aid alignment and help all parts of the organization stretch their contribution, achieving the very most possible, individually and collectively.

- Delivering high performance in a large international organization is a **team game**; the main aim of a planning and accountability framework is to aid alignment (across functions, lines of business, and geographies), create a culture of challenge and stretch, and hold one another to account for both the individual performance and the collective performance.

- A scorecard, irrespective of the number of metrics, will not cover 100 percent of what an organization is aiming to achieve and in particular will not reflect unforeseen challenges and opportunities. **At best it will cover 70 to 80 percent.** Hence, it is wise to keep the number of metrics to a manageable number. The management process still needs to leave room for managers and staff to use their professional judgment.

- The **processes, disciplines, and style of leadership** demonstrated by managers and executives are as important as the actual selection of objectives, metrics, and targets.

Some Myths

There are also a number of myths that need to be cast aside.

People do as they are measured. They do not. Perhaps one-third do, one-third do what they believe is right, and the rest will choose depending on the situation. Hence, the inclusive process of reflection and alignment in selecting the right objectives, metrics, and targets is a critical foundation stone in creating scorecards that are credible for the best people across the organization.

Clear metrics and targets always help. They do not. If they are the wrong ones, we are better off with none. Hence, it is important that your best people are engaged to think through the key performance levers and select metrics that will drive the behaviors you want.

We can adjust leadership style and culture to make a new approach to planning and accountability work. Not so easy. Often you probably cannot. It is essential that the most senior leaders take a lead role in spearheading the implementation of this new approach and buy in fully to the disciplines and behaviors that are implied. Otherwise it will not work.

We can lift metrics and targets from similar organizations and use them. You can't. This is no more true than copying a strategy.

An elegant planning and accountability framework will instantly improve performance. It won't, but it should point you in the right direction.

Good IT systems are an essential ingredient. They are not. Don't start with a technology solution. A good planning and accountability system should feed from existing information and be at a very summary strategic level. It is very likely to draw information from a variety of sources. In due course, once the new framework is refined and well established, it may make sense to take advantage of good software tools. Over time, these might benefit from tighter integration with other key systems, but the business case for this investment may not always be compelling. Importantly, we would like to emphasize that starting with a technology solution will risk the organization being biased or diverted by the needs or limitations of a particular software application rather than devoting energy on the more critical task of designing the right framework with the right metrics, disciplines, and behaviors.

Thorny Issue 1: Useful Metrics for Program Quality and Impact

How can we create a set of consistent metrics at an individual program level? How can performance scores across a range of programs across diverse topics over a wide variety of different political, economic, and social contexts be meaningfully aggregated? These are important challenges, often presented as barriers to the kind of planning and accountability framework that is being put forward and encouraged in this chapter.

The honest answer is that we probably cannot, at least at an absolute level. It is probably not realistic to have a consistent absolute metric or set of metrics for program quality and impact for all programs in all contexts. Hence, it is necessary to find creative and pragmatic ways of designing metrics that are meaningful and helpful and encourage the right behaviors.

In addition, it is worth emphasizing that the implementation of a robust planning and accountability framework does not conflict with the development and strengthening of monitoring and evaluation approaches and systems that are being usefully progressed in many international agencies. A good planning and accountability framework will feed from good monitoring and evaluation processes and systems.

Case Example: Program Metrics
The following case exhibit is an interesting example of how one NGO sought to overcome this challenge, through a pragmatic approach that seeks to achieve three important objectives:

- to create a shared understanding and vision of what makes a quality program,

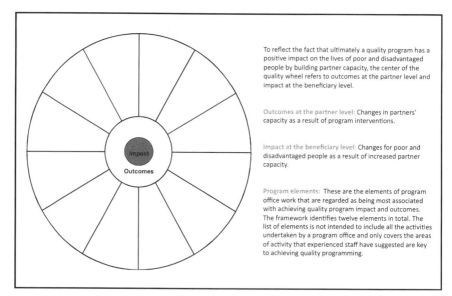

To reflect the fact that ultimately a quality program has a positive impact on the lives of poor and disadvantaged people by building partner capacity, the center of the quality wheel refers to outcomes at the partner level and impact at the beneficiary level.

Outcomes at the partner level: Changes in partners' capacity as a result of program interventions.

Impact at the beneficiary level: Changes for poor and disadvantaged people as a result of increased partner capacity.

Program elements: These are the elements of program office work that are regarded as being most associated with achieving quality program impact and outcomes. The framework identifies twelve elements in total. The list of elements is not intended to include all the activities undertaken by a program office and only covers the areas of activity that experienced staff have suggested are key to achieving quality programming.

Figure 6.6 Quality framework wheel diagram.

- to pull together existing ways of measuring and assessing all of its programs into one coherent whole, and
- to help identify strengths and areas for improvement within and across programs so that relevant management action can be taken to improve program quality.

This is summarized briefly in figure 6.6 and uses what is referred to as the "quality framework wheel diagram." This has "impact" and "outcomes" at the core but also sets out what it regards as the key elements or contributors to a quality program.

For this agency, outcomes are defined at a partner level, that is, changes in partners' capacity as a result of program interventions. Impact is defined at a beneficiary level, that is, changes for poor and disadvantaged people as a result of increased partner capacity. (Clearly, this would vary considerably depending of the nature of the kinds of contributions different NGOs have to offer.) The list of elements is not intended to include all the activities undertaken by a program office and only covers the areas of activity that experienced staff suggested to be the most important to achieving quality programming.

What is particularly attractive for this approach is the use of straight-forward metrics that have a simple range (1–4) in terms of how performance is judged against each element, simply described as follows:

4 Performance exceeds expectations
3 Performance meets expectations
2 Performance partly meets expectations
1 Room for improvement

For each element, each level has a descriptor that sets out what needs to have been achieved to score 1 through 4. The scoring is partly by self-assessment, and field staff are asked to score themselves precisely against the indicators, noting that there may be very good reasons why there may be a low score on a particular indicator. There is the opportunity to add a short narrative to give a brief explanation of the score. The agency believes that this approach has a number of very important features and advantages.

1. The emphasis on self-assessment, albeit with some peer and senior manager review, creates a progressive, learning environment. There is a strong emphasis on self-challenge, sharing and learning and particularly on how pro-grams can be improved in the future.

2. The straightforward scoring system means that it is feasible to aggre-gate scores at a program, country, or regional level and also to allow varia-tions in weighting to give different emphasis over time as desired. However, extreme care is needed in aggregating and reporting aggregate scores, so that the accuracy and honesty of the scoring, as well as the quality of self-challenge and learning that is a central part of the benefit, is not prejudiced. Finally, the information gathered during this process provides a very valuable support to future direction setting, planning, and decision making for the organization.

3. This framework builds on data from monitoring and evaluation systems, as well as from other systems and sources depending on the element in ques-tion. As such, it is a reasonably light administrative burden on those involved, emphasizing the value-added process of reviewing and discussing key data and information that already exists. The intention is not to create lots of new report-ing requirements but simply to pull existing information together into one place.

Thorny Issue 2: Useful Metrics for Local Stakeholder and Beneficiary Input and Feedback

One of the very urgent and difficult issues for many INGOs is the challenge of creating a meaningful communication channel or feedback with the end beneficiaries, local communities, and other local stakeholders. This is a much-debated subject, with many good intentions, though often with far too much of what one could describe as tokenistic efforts.

As mentioned earlier in this chapter, there are a wide variety of important external stakeholders, and it is imperative that there is a way to channel their views to influence the design and implementation of future programs, as well as an ability to provide feedback on the results achieved. There are three points that we would like to make on this challenge.

First, we recognize that what a meaningful channel means in practice will depend on the "development paradigm" of each particular agency. For example, what makes sense for a "rights-based" approach will not be the same for an agency with a "community engagement/empowerment" approach, and will be different for an agency with a "customer service" approach. In the latter case, local beneficiaries and communities can arguably be regarded as clients or customers who have the option to move to another supplier.

Second, as a guide, respecting the considerations indicated above, one could expect that the meaningful input from local stakeholders and beneficiaries should occur at a number of key points in the planning and development process:

1. Input should occur during the development of the local strategic plan for that country by the agency (typically a horizon of five to ten or more years), where the broad program goals and objectives are defined. This analysis and planning should be carried out in tandem with local stakeholders and other local partners.
2. It should occur during the design and implementation stages of each specific program.
3. It should occur as part of the program closure for each program to get a robust view of the perceptions of local stakeholders of how the program has been carried out and contributed compared to expectations.
4. And it should occur at an appropriate period after the end of the program (could be several years) to measure the lasting impact of each program.

It is appreciated that this kind of consultation and input does occur at many of these stages in many international agencies today, but too often it is not as meaningful and systematic as it might be and often not well integrated into planning and decision making.

Next, if metrics in this area are both useful and meaningful to aggregate, they need to be kept fairly simple. Some will already be an integral part of the measurement approach for program quality and impact, as illustrated in the earlier example. In any case, applying a pragmatic 1 to 4 scoring system, similar to the example outlined earlier, may again be a useful approach, again where there is a practical descriptor of what needs to be done to achieve each score.

6.5. Implementation Considerations and Suggestions

As indicated earlier, an integrated planning and accountability framework is one of a number of underpinning components that enable an international organization to function effectively. Hence, it is important to position the implementation in the context of other interdependent dimensions that need to be considered, such as structure, leadership style, and the strength and maturity of other important enabling processes. Some of these dimensions are illustrated in figure 6.7 and include the following:

- **Governance structures; board compositions, skills, and behaviors; and decision-making frameworks:** Some important refinements may well be required, such as refinement of roles and authority of some boards and executive teams, as well as broader decision-making protocols and processes.
- **Management and leadership behaviors and traits:** Old habits are hard to change. However, it is possible that individual managers and leaders will need to adjust their approach to play their part in facilitating an effective planning and accountability framework.
- **Organizational model or structure:** In particular, the openness to some form of matrix structure may be an important ingredient, given that integrated planning and accountability is, in reality, a crosscutting dimension of any international organization.
- **Strengthening of global processes and systems:** In particular, finance, human resources, and monitoring and evaluation are processes that may well need to be strengthened and integrated at a global level.

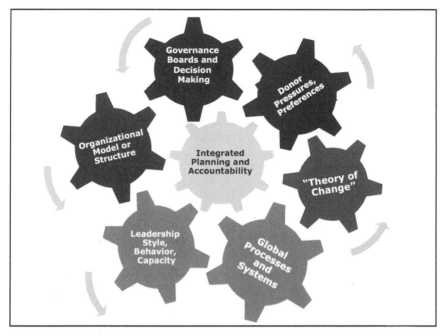

Figure 6.7 Interrelated dimensions of progress.

- **Donor pressures and behaviors:** Donor requirements need to be represented within the planning and accountability process, without requiring a parallel system to be in place that will be expensive and demanding of management time.

Finally, reasonable alignment on a *theory of change* is a very important foundation stone, that is, a shared understanding on how positive lasting change can be brought to poor communities, countries, and regions. If there are major misalignments in this regard, it is unlikely that the implementation of an integrated planning and accountability process can proceed successfully.

Changes to Be Tackled in a Coordinated Manner

At the implementation planning stage, it is important to take good account of changes that may need to be made in parallel, as part of the overall organization-strengthening efforts. However, we appreciate that it is likely that few organizations will have the capacity to do major concurrent strengthening on all of the dimensions in parallel; hence, very careful planning and sequencing will be required.

Typical Challenges and Blockages

When considering implementation across a large INGO, there may be a wide range of issues that need to be taken into account. Some of these are illustrated in figure 6.8, which is an expanded version of the diagram introduced earlier in this chapter. In the preparation for the implementation of a planning and accountability framework, it is essential that these broader issues are uncovered, understood, and dealt with as part of the broader change process.

Success Factors in Implementation

One of the unexpected and valuable benefits of implementing an integrated planning and accountability framework is the opportunity to align some of the best brains in the organization on the most important drivers and levers of value and impact. Clarity and alignment on factors that drive impact maximization, and also how these factors interplay with one another, is an essential route toward selecting the best metrics and targets.

Hence, the participation of the very best people, and the process followed to identify and agree on the levers and targets, is a very important stage in the process of developing metrics and targets. In reality, the best people will, most likely, do what they believe is right; hence, if they are indeed right, it is

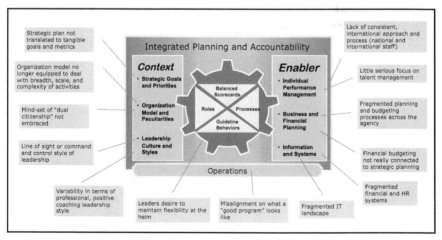

Figure 6.8 Common implementation challenges.

best to reflect that wisdom into the selection of metrics and targets and hence into the collective wisdom of the organization. However, if they are wrong we need to find a way of helping them see a better way.

There are a variety of tools and methods to help think through the most useful and concise set of metrics. One approach is to bring some of the best people together to develop what is referred to as a "causal loop" map, which is built around a clear definition of the long-term impact the agency wants to contribute. This involves qualitative (and sometimes quantitative) mapping of the trade-offs between different levers or choices that contribute to long-term impacts or results. This can be a very effective way of fine-tuning the overall performance of any organization, respecting of course that some intuitive-based judgments may need to be made to complete such a modeling exercise.

In the course of such an approach, setting a "super-stretch mega target" can be a very productive way to clarify the most important levers to get the scalable impact that development agencies are striving to contribute. This kind of approach is productively used during similar efforts in the private sector. I particularly like the "times 2" approach, which says simply, how can we double the bottom-line value of an organization within, say, eighteen to twenty-four months? What would we have to believe and achieve? What levers would you focus on? What metrics would be the most important to emphasize? Similarly, for development and humanitarian agencies, a similar super-stretch target may be an interesting way of stretching the thinking, helping to identify the most important levers and metrics to guide and accelerate future progress.

If required, there is a reasonable amount of useful published material to help with this. A good example is the work of Kaplan and Norton, *Strategy Maps*,[7] which is a useful reference.

Key Stages in the Implementation Process

The following is an outline of one possible approach to implementing an integrated planning and accountability framework for an INGO. This is illustrated in figure 6.9.

0. **Get the right people involved.** While it may sound obvious, it is incredibly important to select the right individuals to lead the effort, individuals who are deeply knowledgeable about the work of the agency, are heavily respected across the organization, and have the ability to navigate the range of challenges and barriers that may emerge. Moreover, it is critical that the CEO and also his leadership team are not only supportive but also active and visible during the implementation process. Now proceed to step 1.

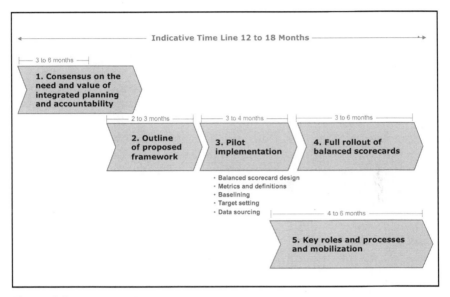

Figure 6.9 Indicative implementation steps.

1. **Gain consensus across the organization for the need, value,** and meaning of a single, integrated global planning and accountability framework. This will require considerable consultation and reflection, preparing the ground for a change in consistency, professionalism, and discipline on how all constituents of the organization plan, track, and manage its performance.

2. **Build an outline of the proposed future accountability framework.** What are the main areas of performance and accountability that might need to be included? What objectives and metrics might be considered for each of these areas? How do these objectives and metrics need to be shaped to facilitate the achievement of the major strategic goals of the organization, as articulated in the current global strategic plan? How do these performance areas cascade across the major constituents of the organization, funding offices, program offices, functions, and program domains? How will the planning and review process work in practice? Who will be involved? What management disciplines need to be changed? How will management and leadership behaviors need to be refined to facilitate effective working of this new approach? How does it connect with the related planning and management processes such as financial planning and budgeting? And how does it connect with career planning and

performance management at an individual level for key roles throughout the organization?

3. Following socialization, discussion, and refinement, **begin formal implementation** for the organization overall, as well as for each of the major constituents of the organization, starting off with some selective pilots. Piloting can be very useful, for example, picking one or two program offices, one or two funding offices, and one or two functions. At every level, the framework will benefit enormously by bringing some of the best brains in the organization, drawn from multiple functions, to develop objectives and indicative targets for each of the performance areas. It is important to reflect on the behaviors that are likely to be encouraged by any particular set of objectives and metrics. This may involve some reflection and modeling of some of the key levers for that part of the organization, considering how these levers combine and interact and especially how they contribute to the ultimate goals of that part of the organization. Unsurprisingly, these key individuals are likely to be the same people who have the deepest understanding of the organization's theory of change, that is, those who have the best insight on how positive and lasting change comes about in developing communities, countries, and regions.

4. Once the framework has been developed and refined, it is then possible to **roll out across all constituents of the organization**. As this is done, it is important to have a coordination and integration process to ensure that objectives, metrics, and targets retain consistency, that is, what we mean by a specific metric or label is the same in different parts of the organization. It is also important to ensure that where metrics cascade down and across the organization, the objectives and targets are coherent. An obvious example of this is that the income-generation target at a global level should be equivalent to an aggregation of the targets across the various constituents of the organization.

5. In parallel with the earlier work, a critical step that requires considerable thought is the **design and mobilization of the key roles** that will be responsible for coordinating, facilitating, and planning the accountability process. It is critical that named, respected individuals are given responsibility for managing the process, both overall and within each major constituent of the organization. In the private sector, there are different approaches taken regarding where these individuals are located within the formal reporting structure of the organization. Increasingly these are being established as very small independent functions (could be a single person), reporting directly to the CEOs of the respective businesses and operating as a network. In other cases they can be attached to the finance functions, in the strategic planning functions, and very occasionally in the HR functions.

The final step, not shown specifically on the chart, is the task of **evolving and improving the design of the balanced scorecards** and the associated roles and processes as the organization learns through experience. It is very likely that well-intentioned efforts in relation to specific metrics yield unexpected and sometimes unhelpful behaviors. However, care should also be taken to maintain as much continuity as possible, to allow the new accountability framework to develop traction and credibility, so the organization can meaningfully track its progress over time.

6.6. Conclusions

The following is a summary of some key points and conclusions that have been raised through this chapter.

1. Integrated planning and accountability is part of the lifeblood of any high-performing international organization. **It is not magic and not rocket science.** However, it requires discipline and professional rigor to implement and operate an approach for any large international organization. It may require a considerable change in the management approach and leadership behaviors.

2. An integrated planning and accountability framework is **one of a number of interconnected dimensions that together facilitate a high-performing INGO.** Other important dimensions include clarity and alignment around strategic goals, the organizational structure, and leadership capacity and behaviors. Important enabling dimensions are financial, human resources, and program monitoring and evaluation processes and systems. If these other dimensions are not working well, the effectiveness of any planning and accountability framework will be considerably diminished.

3. An integrated planning and accountability process is likely to have four main components. First, it should include **a set of consistent balanced scorecards** for all parts of the agency, encompassing objectives, metrics, and targets. Second, it should have some **clear processes** for target setting and monitoring, which are integral parts of the day-to-day management process, and connect with strategic goals, business, and financial planning, as well as individual performance management. Third, it should have clearly **defined roles**, indicating who is involved in facilitating, challenging, or approving target setting and monitoring. Finally, it should have a set of **guidelines around the behaviors** that are encouraged through the planning and accountability process.

4. **External accountability is important and needs to be an integral part of a joined-up planning and accountability approach** not an occasional add-on.

We need to recognize that there are a wide variety of external stakeholders, and their views and feedback need to be meaningfully represented and be relevant in the day-to-day planning and decision-making processes. This is akin to customer feedback mechanisms for any commercial firm. Over time an agency will get more adept at collecting this information in a systematic manner, improving its capacity to use this input more effectively in planning and decision making.

5. A range of newer initiatives such as the International NGO Accountability Charter and the Global Reporting Initiative are extremely useful in drawing attention to external accountability as an important ingredient in the planning and management processes of any international agency. However, the act of producing an annual accountability report that is separate from the real process of day-to-day management is, though useful, not sufficient. There is a risk that it ends up becoming merely a public relations exercise, a parallel sideshow to the real management process, akin to CSR reporting in the early days of corporate dabbling in social responsibility.

6. **Organizational legitimacy will come from a variety of sources** and be nurtured and strengthened over time, through transparency and buy-in to its mission and approach; through transparency and clarity of goals, plans, and progress; through reputation gained in times of need; and hopefully through the appreciation of repeated success in contribution of sustainable progress in the lives of the poor.

The final summary point is this. The idea of **external accountability without strong internal accountability is just not credible.** Without a robust and joined-up planning and performance management process that brings together the contributions of all parts of an international agency, any discussion about external accountability to partners, stakeholders, and beneficiaries risks being merely hollow talk.

Notes

1. J. Crowley and C. Alzaga, *Connecting Business and Development: The "Rubik's Cube" of Cross-Sector Collaboration* (Crowley Institute, July 2009).

2. Morgana Ryan, Shaun Richardson, and Paul Voutier, *Business in Development Study 2012* (Business for Millennium Development and Accenture, on behalf of Australian Agency for International Development, September 2012), www.b4md.com.au.

3. www.ingoaccountabilitycharter.org.

4. Cranfield Research, *The BP Experience* (Cranfield, UK: Cranfield University School of Management, 2002).

5. Robert S. Kaplan and David P. Norton, *The Balanced Scorecard* (Boston, MA: Harvard Business School Press, 1996).

6. Robert S. Kaplan and David P. Norton, "The Balanced Scorecard: Measures That Drive Performance," *Harvard Business Review* (January–February 1992): 71–79.

7. Robert S. Kaplan and David P. Norton, *Strategy Maps: Converting Intangible Assets Into Tangible Outcomes* (Boston, MA: Harvard Business School Press, 1996).

What Does All This Mean?

7.1. A Synopsis

The previous six chapters covered a lot of ground. Throughout, we sought to be frank about the key issues, to challenge those in charge of large international agencies, but also to be pragmatic and constructive in terms of our recommendations and suggestions. However, as for large established and successful incumbents in any industry, there are many reasons to resist change.

In chapter 1, we tackled a set of issues around organizational effectiveness and made twelve suggestions spanning three broad themes, namely, program legitimacy, operational maturity, and credible leadership and governance.

Program legitimacy is anchored first and foremost on the quality and impact of local programs. This is can be helped by creative reflection and alignment on a *theory of change*, providing a basis for a robust and consistent set of program interventions, adapted to local contexts, so that an agency can do the best that it can do, each place it works, all of the time. Most large agencies know deep down that a proportion of their programs are exceptionally good and have a high chance of lasting impact, but there may also be a proportion that are less convincing in terms of effectiveness, scale, or sustainability if scrutinized by the best collective wisdom of the entire organization. As Warren Buffett has been known to remark in relation to his portfolio of investment opportunities, "Why would I invest in my hundredth-most attractive opportunity when I could instead invest more in my favorite one, or at least in one of my top five?" Under the theme of program legitimacy, we also emphasized the need to be able to implement interventions at regional and international levels to complement local efforts, since some of the important blockages to progress go well beyond the scope of national boundaries. Finally, we suggested that agencies need to be much more rigorous in defining what their *core competencies* really are or need to become so they can proactively nurture these competencies for the future and also so they can be much clearer when it makes sense to partner with others.

Regarding **operational maturity**, we discussed the thorny area of international processes and systems. We recognized that one needs to be pragmatic in terms of which processes and systems need to be harmonized and to what extent, as this has the potential to be a time-consuming and expensive task, particularly for organizations covering such a very broad scope of geographies and domains. However, when it comes to basic aspects such as financial management, human resource management, monitoring and evaluation, and knowledge management, it is inconceivable to be able to operate as an effective global organization unless policies, standards, processes, and systems are harmonized to a meaningful degree. We highlighted the need for an integrated approach to planning, management, and accountability, a basic requirement for any high-performing global organization—and one that we feel is an area of considerable weakness for many INGOs. Deficiencies in this area can be an important contributor to the unhelpful "relational" style of management, characterized by a "line of sight," "command and control" approach, which is still a prominent feature in some organizations. Operational maturity also needs to embrace some intangible issues. For example, we believe that being comfortable with the idea of dual citizenship is a core requirement of becoming a coherent, high-performing global organization, where people feel as much a citizen of the global organization as they do of their own country office or function. This issue is a considerable impediment for many INGOs where historic structures and habits still prevail.

The third theme highlighted was **credible leadership and governance.** This has a number of important strands. One is the need to move away from a "North–South" power imbalance, a feature that is stubbornly ingrained in many international agencies, fueled by the decades of history of a North–South resource transfer model of development. Change also needs to permeate governance structures and management composition. There needs to be deliberate effort to unify staff development and career opportunities for all *national, expat, and international* staff. Rather reluctantly, we also tackle the issues and choices around organization structure. This is an area that often gets more attention than one would like; however, given the nature, scope, and scale of international NGOs, we believe that the continuing prevalence of a simple line structure, often geographically based, is no longer equipped for the demands of such a complex range of activities. We believe that a carefully designed matrix structure with a clear set of rules around decision making, enabled by an effective planning and accountability framework, deserves serious consideration. We propose the adoption of a virtual approach to global centers and headquarters, arguing strongly that the global center need not be a single place: instead it should be a set of roles and responsibilities that can be taken on by the most appropriate individuals, wherever they sit in an organization. The concept of a large global center in a Northern city, be it London, Washington, or Geneva, is in our view a barrier to, not a facilitator of, an effective and coherent global organization. We tackle the "old chestnut" of regional roles and structures, arguing for a more thoughtful approach to smaller, more relevant regional hubs that are better able to meet the needs of local programs and people. Finally, meaningful progress around credible global leadership and governance has little chance of success unless there is a single global leadership team that has the mandate to plan and to make timely decisions on behalf of all stakeholders, internally and externally.

A number of the suggestions made in chapter 1 were taken further in subsequent chapters. Chapter 2 takes a deeper look at the idea of *core competence* and explores how this rich idea, as first introduced into the management literature by Prahalad and Hamel[1] in 1990, can provide a very useful lens to explore what core competence is today for INGOs, or indeed could or should be in the future. Chapter 3 takes a deeper look at the issues and options around organizational structure. In this chapter we also cover the idea of organization glue, making an important distinction between the two types of glue, "enabling" and "motivating." Too often major change initiatives pay insufficient attention to the latter. Chapter 4 explores the enormous opportunity provided by ICT4D (information and communications technology for development). We explore what it can bring but also challenge whether these new possibilities will provide a helpful "sustaining" role for large incumbent INGOs or, alternatively, whether they could be a "disruptive" technology that could lead to their ultimate demise, and lean on the insightful ideas of Clayton Christensen from the excellent book *The Innovator's Dilemma.*[2] Chapter 5 looks at the challenge of conducting a strategic planning review, describing some of the key requirements of an effective approach, as well as providing some suggestions and advice for anyone charged with leading such a review. Chapter 6 takes a deeper look at the missing link of "integrated planning and accountability," first highlighted in chapter 1. This chapter develops what we mean by an integrated planning and accountability framework and sets out some practical suggestions on how to implement such a framework.

7.2. Why Should International NGOs Embrace Change?

So why do these ideas and suggestions really matter? Simply, we believe that the status quo is not sustainable. In fact, it is a high-risk situation for many INGOs. In our opinion, evolution toward a stronger, more focused, and coherent international organization is not necessarily a differentiator; it will be a basic requirement to stay relevant in the years ahead. There are two primary lines of argument behind this view.

First, there is an urgent need to create **coherent, connected, and interdependent international organizations** that are able to support larger and more impactful programs at local, regional, and international levels. This should facilitate a number of important benefits:

1. to be more internationally coherent in an increasingly interconnected world
2. to dramatically improve program quality and impact, everywhere an agency operates, through more disciplined use of its best insight and methodology
3. to reduce the risk of failed programs through poor program design and implementation, resulting in fewer worries around reputation risk
4. to be able to support large-scale multinational and international interventions to complement local or national programs
5. to exploit economies of scale and scope in terms of know-how, relationships, processes and systems, and avoiding reinvention
6. to embrace new sets of relationships with new and different partners at an international level, for example, in the area of ICD4D
7. to make timely, tough, and binding decisions at a global level in relation to all of the above and particularly in light of the rapidly changing external and internal context

This does not mean creating a large bureaucratic structure that sits on top of and weighs down local country structures. It does mean weaving a coherent set of global responsibilities across the organization so that it is more joined up, more disciplined, and more deliberate in everything it does.

Second, there is an equally important need for local country organizations to become much **more capable, independent, and vibrant independent actors** within their national context while leveraging the advantages of being part of an international interconnected agency in terms of knowledge, knowhow, professionalism, and reputation. In reality, all too often country-based offices remain overly dependent branches of fund-raising offices in the North, often subscale and unsustainable. There are a number of important drivers for this change:

1. to be able to generate significant amounts of their own resources, either locally or through donors who want to fund credible local agencies and programs
2. to be effective local advocates for change, within the local development context and with a credible degree of local independence

3. to be able to be credible partners at national and local levels with government bodies, local private sector organizations, and other local civil society organizations
4. to be sustainable in a world where there may be little or no economic growth in so-called developed economies who traditionally provided much of the funding, where donors have a desire to be much more locally connected, and where future programs are centered more around state strengthening and policy changes and less around service delivery

For a number of large international organizations, their score in either of the two respects described above is simply not good enough. They are not effective, interconnected, and coherent organizations, on the one hand, and their country offices are not capable, credible, and vibrant actors for local change, on the other. This is not a sustainable model. There is much talk in the sector around the challenge of "disintermediation." This is a real threat for organizations that are little more than expensive funnels for transmitting funds and resources from loosely connected offices in the North to loosely connected dependent program offices in the South. However, we strongly believe that risk is less worrying for organizations that are truly coherent and capable at both local and international levels.

What does it mean for the poor and disadvantaged? This is the crunch question. In short it should mean significantly better, much larger, and far more innovative programs that are able to leverage the best brains across an international organization in terms of how they are designed and implemented. Greater international coherence and connections should mean that there is far more informed scrutiny on program selection at the outset, with weaker programs being set aside, allowing greater resources to be invested in programs that are likely to contribute more.

This should result in a higher-quality, more focused, and more consolidated portfolio of programs, with a considerably larger average size or footprint. This should also simplify the work of tracking outputs and impact. Programs will be designed at the outset with carefully thought-out research questions and disciplined baseline data allowing for more meaningful assessment of impact. This should help attract more and larger streams of funding and resources to support the most productive new opportunities. All of this is good news for those who really matter.

What does it mean for staff? For staff who work in INGOs throughout the world, the opportunity is considerable. In addition to their day-to-day

roles at local levels, they should feel that they are also part of a strong global effort to deliver large-scale contributions at national, regional, and international
levels (the idea of dual citizenship). Their individual skills, expertise, and career
development will be boosted by their participation and contribution through
meaningful new ways, for example, by opportunities provided through global
lines of business and experience. In these new dimensions, they can interact
with, learn from, and contribute to their peers throughout the world in the
design and implementation of programs. They will feel that they are part of a
vibrant global knowledge management network that is facilitated by a strong
connection with their peers wherever they work. They will also benefit from
more consistent and systematic procedures for knowledge capture and dis-
semination.

Their career development will benefit from the best training and knowledge available across the organization. Their performance evaluation will be
based on combined inputs from their local line management, as well as from
leaders of the global lines of expertise who are most relevant to their technical area. As they build up deeper expertise, they will have the opportunity to
stretch themselves and to contribute even more. Importantly, talented national
staff in developing countries who in the past have felt the frustration of hitting
a glass ceiling in terms of career opportunities can also become *dual citizens*
and contribute beyond their local geographies, even if they continue to work
in their local country. This is all good news for the most talented and ambi-
tious people. What is equally important, all of this will provide more transparency to expose poor performance, stimulating those who are not performing
well to improve or to exit.

7.3. A Few Thoughts on Navigating Change

As discussed in chapter 6, there are a number of dimensions that need to progress in tandem to achieve a high-performing global organization. These are set
out in figure 7.1 and are a simplified lens on the twelve recommendations and
suggestions set out in chapter 1. As we highlight these important and interconnected areas, we appreciate that implementing wholesale change in parallel
across all dimensions may be neither affordable nor realistic. Hence, careful
prioritization and sequencing of change is paramount.

However, once an international agency is aligned on the need to make
significant improvements, pace is important as staff across the organization
will soon expect demonstrable evidence of progress in terms of benefits both
for the poor and also for their own careers. Once the need for change and the

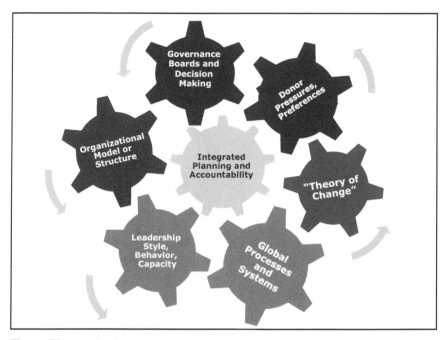

Figure 7.1 Interrelated dimensions of progress.

understanding of the new vision become understood and accepted, it is very important to move quickly. It is all too easy to underestimate the ability of staff throughout an organization to embrace change. It is also important to minimize the fear or the uncertainty created when the new vision is communicated. This can be helped by early and decisive steps that allow staff and managers to move quickly into the new world and not get frozen in uncertainty as they wait for new changes to take place.

As we reflect on the importance of sequencing, what might be the best approach? A number of the required changes may, by their nature, take some considerable time to bear fruit. Changes that harmonize policies and standards can take several months to implement, even years in some cases. Work to harmonize processes and systems can take even longer, sometimes up to two, three years—sometimes longer.

What about changes to leadership style, behaviors, and capacity? Most agree that this is an absolutely critical contributor to the change that needs to take place, not just for the cadre of leaders at the top but also for leaders at every level throughout an organization. There are many aspects to leadership to dissect that are beyond the scope of this book. However, when we reflect on what we have observed in many agencies, we believe that many of the issues are heavily influenced by context. By this we mean that a number of the challenges in leadership behavior are a result of the natural stresses and pressures and characteristics of the environment within large INGOs. However, some early and deliberate action is advisable. For example, some early efforts to define and communicate the kinds of leadership behaviors that are expected and are to be encouraged can be a very useful first step. It can be very visible and signal the dawning of a new direction, which should hopefully be welcomed by staff across the organization and also by external stakeholders. Desired leadership behaviors can also be embedded in the individual performance management processes, as discussed in chapter 6. This can be helped, for example, by the introduction of a 360 feedback survey, allowing leaders throughout the organization to get honest and helpful feedback.

Hence, when we consider all of the above, we believe it makes sense to start with (1) those changes that are the quickest to do and are the most visible throughout the organization and (2) the changes that can help facilitate or accelerate a range of other improvements that will, unavoidably, take a number of years to follow through. Hence, we argue that changes to organizational models and structure are steps to be taken at an early stage of the process, since they can often be implemented relatively quickly and they signify important changes in responsibility, priority, and power. This should also help to make the necessary and tough decisions that will be required for the broader change process to be successful. Changes in governance structures and formal decision-making rights link closely with changes in structure, and by their nature can sometimes take time. However, if boards are serious about leading, driving, and supporting the changes that are needed throughout the organization, why not start with early, decisive, and demonstrable changes at this level at the earliest opportunity?

7.4. The Sector in 2024

How might the sector look in 2024? There are many well-discussed external trends that are expected to have a considerable impact over the coming decade, issues such as shifting geopolitics, climate change, population growth, continuing urbanization, pressures on natural resources (fresh water in particular), and growing inequality, to name but a few. The exact impact of this combination of pressures is harder to predict, as is the likely trajectory of the global economy following the extraordinary financial crisis that started in

2008. After five years of turmoil, many are predicting that we may see at least another decade of static or declining real growth in many of the largest developed economies. All of this will place considerable pressures on the flows of aid, causing major new strains on the future architecture of the development and humanitarian sectors. This is, of course, not taking account of the more extreme risks mankind could face from the famous "five horsemen of the apocalypse" from the book of Revelation (famine, plague, migration, war, state failure), as revisited in Ian Morris's excellent account of the history of development over the past ten thousand years, *Why the West Rules—For Now.*[3]

Let's look at one hypothetical scenario for 2024. The aid architecture has been dramatically transformed by 2024. There are now three established domains attracting attention. These are (the proportion of aid investment budgets in parentheses) infrastructure and trade (60 percent), disaster and disaster preparedness (30 percent), and social development, primarily education and health (10 percent). Rolling five-year programs are developed for each of the three domains at local, national, and subregional levels, in close collaboration with national governments, the World Bank, and other high-level expert bodies. Program planners and architects are appointed for each area and appoint companies and agencies to implement components of programs at local, national, and regional levels. Those who design and have oversight are excluded from competing for implementation contracts. As an example, the program manager for infrastructure and trade in central and east Africa is a consortium that is led by Ove Arup and also includes CNOC, Tata Consulting Engineers, and two local African NGOs.

The aid flows are now very different. The biggest area by far is infrastructure and trade, attracting the majority of investment money and now accelerating investment into roads, rail, and fiber-optic networks, as well as helping poorer countries address trade barriers and other aspects of their economic fabric. Key officials from government ministries are strongly represented on the steering of all the major programs, and every effort is made to align the content of future investment programs with national development plans. However, all programs attracting external investment are independently governed and managed and are highly transparent, with clear goals and success metrics. The average project in each of the three program areas is unrecognizably larger than it was ten years ago, but there are far fewer in number.

The concept of *direct budget transfer* has now been largely abandoned—prompted by growing evidence that it weakened rather than strengthened local government capacity of poorer countries and also by fears that the risk of corruption was just too much. A number of scandals first came to light in 2012 and then snowballed over the subsequent years as public scrutiny increased. The concept of charitable giving still exists but has evolved dramatically as the general public and institutions increasingly think of themselves as social investors, releasing their funds to selected programs, with the clear intention to get their money back and even, in certain cases, to get some return on their investment. Where this is not possible, the concept of social return on investment has now evolved to become a normal part of the parlance of development discourse, particularly in the area of social development. Thankfully, the old question of "How much of my $10 goes to the poor?" seems like a question from a bygone age.

The landscape of the thirty largest INGOs in the world in 2024 is very different from that in 2013. Only two remain in a recognizable form, and these are less important players than they were. A dramatically changing development, political, and economic context, combined with severe financial pressures, resulted in three mega mergers among eleven of the top agencies between 2018 and 2021, the largest bringing together five long-established INGOs into one combined entity, though structured internally into three semi-independent divisions to align with the three established investment domains of trade and infrastructure, humanitarian interests, and social development as outlined previously. A number decided to focus on one domain or subdomain such as health or education. A few decided to concentrate their attention on specific microregions, reducing their geographical span from more than seventy-plus countries down to a handful and in some cases just one country, becoming close partners with governments and other local stakeholders in that geography in the pursuit of a clear set of focused development goals.

Clearly, this prediction is almost certain to be wrong! However, that is not the point. The idea that the context that INGOs currently work in will be unchanged in 2024 is equally unlikely. What is sure is that INGOs need to reinvent themselves to stay relevant in the years ahead.

Notes

1. C. K. Prahalad and Gary Hamel, "The Core Competence of the Corporation," *Harvard Business Review* (May–June 1990): 79–90.

2. Clayton M. Christensen, *The Innovator's Dilemma: When New Technologies Cause Great Firms to Fail* (Boston, MA: Harvard Business School Press, 1997).

3. Ian Morris, *Why the West Rules—For Now* (New York: Picador, 2011); *The Patterns of History and What They Reveal About the Future* (London, Profile Books Ltd, 2010).

Index

About the Authors

James Crowley is a business advisor with more than twenty-five years of experience in a variety of large private sector companies and more recently with a range of agencies in the international development sector.

James joined Accenture's strategic consulting practice in 1989, became a partner in 1997, and worked across a range of strategy and organization change assignments for energy, consumer products, high tech, and public sector companies, working with major international clients such as SmithKline Beecham, Hewlett-Packard, Shell, British Gas, and a raft of energy companies. Up to 2005, James led Accenture's strategy practice in the United Kingdom and Ireland and was the practice lead for the European Mergers, Acquisitions, and Alliances practice for many years.

James formally left Accenture's commercial consulting practice in 2005 to focus on strategic and organizational performance issues in the international development sector. However, he has continued to work extensively with Accenture's not-for-profit practice, Accenture Development Partnerships. Over that time, he has led a range of assignments on international strategic issues for clients such as Plan International, AMREF, World Vision, Amnesty International, and Voluntary Services Overseas.

In parallel with his ongoing advisory work, James invests a proportion of his time in new independent research pieces that aim to stimulate new management ideas around the effectiveness of large international NGOs, as well as stimulate new collaborative approaches between development and private sector organizations. The first of these was released in 2009, in collaboration with World Vision and Accenture Development Partnerships, titled *The "Rubik's Cube" of Cross-Sector Collaboration* (www.thecrowleyinstitute.org).

James holds a first-class honors degree in engineering from University College Cork, a master's degree in offshore engineering from University College London, and an MBA from London Business School.

Morgana Ryan is the Asia Pacific Director for Accenture Development Partnerships and has experience in a range of strategic, business process, and IT assignments spanning the private and development sectors.

Morgana joined Accenture in 1997, and for a number of years her primary focus was working with large utility and international oil companies, including EnergyAustralia, TransAlta, and Shell Exploration and Production. This gave her the opportunity to work in Australia, the Middle East, Europe, Asia, and Africa.

In recent years she has dedicated her focus on the international development sector, applying her skills and experiences with Accenture Development Partnerships, a not-for-profit organization within Accenture. She has been privileged to work with some of the world's largest international NGOs at multiple levels, designing and implementing improvements at international headquarters, secretariats, and national organizations at regional and country levels. This work has largely focused on how complex international NGOs with limited resources can operate to achieve more together, particularly when faced with significant geographic and programmatic footprints. Recent clients include Oxfam International, Amnesty International, Plan International, Save the Children, and Catholic Relief Services.

While working on these projects, Morgana was struck by how little literature is available on operational and structural aspects of managing international NGOs at a practical level in the quest for better organizational performance. On this basis Morgana and James Crowley sought to collaborate to share their commercial and development sector experiences as a reference for those working in international development.

Morgana holds a first-class honors degree in economics from Monash University, Clayton, Australia.